D1637418

Every new manager makes mistakes. But you might make fewer of them if you follow the practical advice that Ryan Hawk has spent years collecting.

—ADAM GRANT, Professor of Management at the Wharton School of the University of Pennsylvania, *New York Times* bestselling author of *Originals* and *Give and Take*, and host of the TED podcast *WorkLife*

Welcome to Management by Ryan Hawk is more than a guide on how to effectively lead people. It will force you to look inward and rethink how you learn, grow, and improve. If you want to scale up your leadership ability, you must read this book.

—VERNE HARNISH, founder of the Entrepreneurs' Organization and bestselling author of *Scaling Up*

Greatness is in the agency of others. The transition from player to coach is a drastic one, but Hawk's accessible, practical read will help new managers learn what it takes to move from being responsible for their own success to being responsible for the success of many.

—SCOTT GALLOWAY, Professor of Marketing at NYU Stern School of Business and bestselling author of *The Four* and *The Algebra of Happiness*

If you are curious and open for the ride, you will discover that leadership is a journey into yourself. Ryan Hawk is someone who points the way, illustrating how you can't lead a team or a company until you first learn to lead yourself. Ryan offers inspiring and practical advice based on his lessons as a sports and business athlete and by sharing insights he's learned from others along the way.

—BETH COMSTOCK, former Vice Chair of GE and bestselling author of *Imagine It Forward*

A superb script for sustained success, *Welcome to Management* is the perfect playbook for leaders who want to go to the next level.

—JAMES KERR, bestselling author of *Legacy*

Ryan Hawk is that rarest of people—a truly curious soul who asks questions that drill down into the heart of the matter, leave space for contemplation, and gently urge his subjects to look inside for answers they might not yet have discovered themselves.

—ROBERT KURSON, *New York Times* bestselling author of *Shadow Divers*

New managers face a steep learning curve and an entirely new landscape of opportunity and responsibility. With this book, Ryan has created a resource for the day-to-day tactics of great leaders. Don't miss out on this incredible companion for managers who aspire to lead strong teams to extraordinary outcomes.

> —SCOTT BELSKY, Founder and CEO of Behance and author of
> *The Messy Middle*

The same traits that brought Ryan Hawk success as an athlete and business leader—curiosity, self-awareness, commitment—make him an indispensable guide to the crucial and often challenging transition from player to leader. By reading *Welcome to Management*, you'll be standing on the shoulders of the hundreds of legendary business leaders whose wisdom Hawk has distilled.

> —ALEX HUTCHINSON, bestselling author of *Endure*

If you are new to a leadership role, then this book has the power to take years off your learning curve. If you have been leading a team forever, then the depth of experience in this read will make you wonder how you made it this far without it and will empower you to raise your game to a new level.

> —PHIL JONES, author of *Exactly What to Say*

A thorough, well-researched, and highly practical manual for new managers. When you promote someone, first congratulate them, and then immediately hand them a copy of this book.

> —TODD HENRY, author of *Herding Tigers*

Ryan Hawk offers much needed practical advice to help tackle the challenges ahead for new managers. It is especially valuable as you realize the hard truth that being good at a job doesn't directly translate into being successful at leading others to do it. Learning that hard truth, and discovering Ryan's response to it, make it worth your while to buy this book.

> —ANNIE DUKE, bestselling author of *Thinking in Bets*

Ryan Hawk uses his unique knowledge and understanding of leadership to help the reader learn practical ways to lead, to build the right culture, and to improve each day. Ryan uses great examples to deliver his message, and after reading this book, I am ready to enact his words of wisdom.

> —MICHAEL LOMBARDI, three-time Super Bowl–winning
> executive and author of *Gridiron Genius*

A no-nonsense book from a no-nonsense guy about the challenges and opportunities of leadership, drawn from experience and failure and the best of what others have figured out.

—BRENT BESHORE, CEO of adventur.es and author of
The Messy Marketplace

From the time he was a young high school and collegiate quarterback to the present, Ryan Hawk has always had the passion to serve and to lead. His presentations, podcasts, and now his book will make a difference in many lives.

—JIM TRESSEL, former National Champion Ohio State
University football coach and President of Youngstown
State University

WELCOME TO
MANAGEMENT

WELCOME TO
MANAGEMENT

How to Grow from

Top Performer to

Excellent Leader

RYAN HAWK

New York   Chicago   San Francisco   Athens   London   Madrid
Mexico City   Milan   New Delhi   Singapore   Sydney   Toronto

2 3 4 5 6 7 8 9   LCR   24 23 22 21 20

ISBN: 978-1-260-45805-3
MHID: 1-260-45805-9

e-ISBN: 978-1-260-45807-7
e-MHID: 1-260-45807-5

Library of Congress Cataloging-in-Publication Data

Names: Hawk, Ryan, author.
Title: Welcome to management : how to grow from top performer to excellent leader / by
    Ryan Hawk.
Description: New York : McGraw-Hill Education, [2020] | Includes bibliographical references
    and index.
Identifiers: LCCN 2019031907 (print) | LCCN 2019031908 (ebook) | ISBN 9781260458053
    (hardcover) | ISBN 9781260458077 (ebook)
Subjects: LCSH: Management. | Leadership.
Classification: LCC HD31.2 .H365 2020 (print) | LCC HD31.2 (ebook) | DDC 658.4/092—dc23
LC record available at https://lccn.loc.gov/2019031907
LC ebook record available at https://lccn.loc.gov/2019031908

McGraw-Hill Education books are available at special quantity discounts to use as premiums and sales promotions or for use in corporate training programs. To contact a representative, please visit the Contact Us pages at www.mhprofessional.com.

To Mom and Pistol—

my past, present, and future models

for excellent leadership—

thank you

CONTENTS

PART I
LEAD YOURSELF

FOREWORD

Navigation is especially challenging when your destination isn't just unknown—it's unknowable.

One of the first things you learn in the Army is land navigation. In fact, I learned it before I ever set foot on the battlefield; it is a mandatory course at West Point. Land navigation sounds incredibly challenging (and it is), but its core principle is simple: soldiers must learn to follow a route through unfamiliar landscapes with tools no more sophisticated than a compass.

Learning about land navigation is critical for a number of reasons. In an environment where armies fight symmetrically on the battlefield, knowing your position (and seeking to ascertain your opponent's) allows each side to create complicated and precise plans for striking their opponents. Land navigation also helps to build strong teams, as each soldier works toward a shared objective. Perhaps most important, with the changing nature of warfare, land navigation helps us to orient ourselves in a world without the luxury of the Internet or the GPS.

The key to land navigation is to constantly be aware of your position in relation to your destination. This is not easy, given that your position is shifting at any given moment. Critically, these steps require a map. Without knowledge of where we stand, the world around us, and where we are hoping to go, we run the risk of wandering without a purpose. In this sense, land navigation is not entirely unlike leadership—there are many paths to reach an ultimate destination. But how can we know where to go without a map?

I have spent most of my life studying leadership. It was the core of my time at West Point, my career in the Army, and the beginnings of my time as a founder of McChrystal Group. With every new challenge, I reflected on my values and the paths of those who had come before me. In so doing, I thought that I was as much of an expert on leadership as there could be. Society seemed to agree; I have been blessed with modest success. During my command in Iraq and Afghanistan, I faced many tough decisions, but my team and I scored more victories than we ever expected. Nine years ago, I began teaching a course on leadership at Yale University's Jackson Institute for Global Affairs, a course I continue to teach today. McChrystal Group has created new methodologies for developing leadership in the private sector.

I know how unbelievably lucky I am, but I also believe that my leadership has played a role in my triumphs. I am a skilled land navigator, and I spent my career successfully leading teams toward our destination. However, in writing my memoirs, I began to recognize that the path to my destination has required many diversions. As I drilled down to the details of my time in the Army, I began to see how my successes truly came to be. Even in my own story, I found myself to be a supporting character, not wholly responsible for the achievements my team has attained. Rather, in looking back, it was clear that our focus on adaptability was key. Depending on the context of a given moment, my job (and my role as a leader) shifted based on the needs of my teammates.

In the time since I published *My Share of the Task*, I have started to reformulate what it means to be a good leader, an effective leader, and the best leader that I could be. All of this broad and philosophical thinking helped me to realize that leadership isn't what we think it is—and it never has been.

Leadership is not something I learned in the classroom and implemented over the course of my life. It has been a product of the relationships that I have made throughout my life. There was no map that would have led me to take the route from a young cadet to my current life in Alexandria, Virginia. Only with the benefit of hindsight can I see the true nature of where I have traveled, and the means by which I have become the person that I am. At any given moment in my life, it was an internal compass that guided me only to my true north.

Perhaps, then, leadership is about building a path for ourselves; and more critically, leadership is accepting the fact that starting that trip with any idea of where we will end up may be a fool's errand. We can always aspire to grow into the leader that we envision ourselves becoming, but we cannot rely on an existing map to tell us how to get there. If we could, then it would be easy for us all to determine the traits, actions, and choices that will set us on the path to virtuous leadership. However, given that we each find ourselves uniquely positioned in our own lives, there are no common mapped-out routes that every person must take to get where we hope to go.

Leaders are less like navigators in that way, and more like cartographers. We carve our own path forward into the future, knowing that we cannot predict what lies ahead. This uncertainty is exciting—we should not be afraid in facing a world of possibility. Rather, we should be emboldened by the knowledge that while we can learn from the paths that others have pioneered, the route we map is entirely our own. We are navigating a new world, one that no one else has seen through our eyes. The journey that we ultimately take creates the person that we become—this journey is the path of our leadership.

BUT WHERE TO BEGIN?

The question is a daunting one, to be sure. The book that you are reading, *Welcome to Management* by Ryan Hawk, is a remarkably good place to start. His work provides nuanced and articulate insights into the best way to begin developing a plan for bringing to light how we should lead—and it starts with reexamining ourselves.

When cartographers begin their voyage to the unfamiliar, they begin with what they can identify and observe; they situate themselves in the world by looking to what they know best. As Ryan identifies, in developing our path toward leadership, we must begin with ourselves, both inside and out. Only then can we begin to build our teams, lead our teams, and ultimately seek to have our leadership stand the test of time.

It should be said that cartography is an onerous task, and one that has fallen out of fashion, as Ryan aptly notes. We rely on technology to point us in the right direction; in the same way, we shirk the kinds of profound thought that force us to grapple with who we truly are. Today's society, no matter how complex and machine-driven it may be, requires leadership more than ever. It takes courage to be a cartographer; while it is hard work, it is the right work.

In that vein, writing on leadership today is a special kind of challenge. With every week, new books appear on the shelves, claiming to have the one true method for becoming a good leader. Few books revel in the process of leadership, though, the experience of what it means to grow into a leadership role. As you read *Welcome to Management*, think about what it means to be a successful leader in your own mind. Analyze the eventual payoff that he discusses, and how it looks in your mind. And most important, make the conscious decision not to rely only on the roads traveled by others—as Ryan writes, your journey begins with you.

After you finish this book, you will have many ideas about how to begin growing into the leader that Ryan discusses. When you do, I have one piece of advice: put down the map, and pick up the compass. I can't wait to see where you'll go.

General Stanley McChrystal
U.S. Army (Ret.)

INTRODUCTION

Ancora imparo. (Yet, I am learning.)*
—MICHELANGELO

Jennifer materialized in the doorway of my brand-new office without a sound. I nearly jumped when I looked up and saw her standing there. Her pursed lips struggled to keep her face from spilling the emotion that was clearly damned up. It wasn't good. It was my first week as a manager—my first week having an office with *walls* and a door that closed, not to mention a big window and a fancy Herman Miller chair.

What did I do? Thoughts of self-doubt welled up in me. I had been promoted to lead the team that I had been a member of just days earlier. *She's probably upset they chose me, or she thinks I don't deserve it, that I'm too young, too inexperienced. Could she be right? I'm only 27, and she started her career when I was in grade school.*

"Oh! Hey, Jennifer. What's—" I didn't get to finish.

"Ryan, my husband cheated on me," she said. Her voice quivered. "He wants . . . a divorce."

What? If this moment had a soundtrack, Jennifer's words would've cut the music with a giant record-scratch. *Why is she telling me this? What am I supposed to do?* My mind reeled. I couldn't imagine divulging this kind of information to my boss (especially someone I only knew casually as a peer a few days ago), let alone having any clue what to do when I was the "boss" getting it dropped in my lap. I had not counted

---

* *Ancora imparo* is an Italian phrase meaning "Yet, I am learning." It is often attributed to the Renaissance genius Michelangelo, supposedly observed by him at the age of 87.

on this kind of conversation in my new leadership role. Nobody told me that a manager would have to deal with situations like this.

Welcome to management.

If you are holding this book because you've just been promoted and are in a new management position, congratulations. You are now the subject of the dinner table conversations of every person who reports to you. You have become the individual your employees complain about to their spouses and children. You are now responsible for the careers of those who report to you. You are now "the boss." Did you realize what your manager did when you were an individual contributor? Did you think they had it easy?

If you're like I was, you probably couldn't wait to get your promotion and become the boss. Unfortunately, you don't fully appreciate everything management entails until it's your job to do.

With Jennifer standing there, waiting for me to respond, I quickly realized there was so much more to leading a team than I had previously thought. In that moment, it dawned on me: I wasn't sure what a manager actually *did*.

THE FIRST PROMOTION

I grew up professionally in sales organizations. Telephonic sales was my first "real" job after my arena football career ended, and I was focused on figuring out how to win. For me, winning meant not just consistently hitting my sales quota, but staying at the top of the sales rep stack rankings.

After making my mark for several years, my success as an individual contributor earned me the opportunity to interview for a leadership role. With the leadership skills I developed as a Division 1 college and professional quarterback, I was certain I was ready. Then I had my conversation with Jennifer, and I realized I had to learn an entirely new way of operating if I wanted to avoid becoming the latest proof that the Peter Principle is quite real.

The Peter Principle is a concept in management developed by Laurence J. Peter, which observes that people in a hierarchy tend to rise to their "level of incompetence."[1] Employees are promoted based on their success in previous jobs until they reach a level at which they are no longer competent, as their skills in one job do not necessarily translate to another. Though an employee may be a high performer in one area, managing others to do the job is a wholly different skill set—one dependent on the ability to *lead* more than on the ability to *perform*. In other words, the fact that you were a top performer in your previous role does not guarantee that you have the skills to become an effective manager. That said, you are more likely to be promoted into a management role because of your high performance. Kind of a Catch-22, isn't it?

I've always had an interest in performance excellence and leadership. Having grown up as an athlete, I spent much of my formative years learning how to work with others in a team setting. I've been on winning teams and on losing teams, and both experiences taught me about the tactics and psychology it takes to sustain excellence. Despite these experiences, it was still difficult to know exactly how to put all of this into action when I became a manager for the first time.

My story is not an anomaly. Few first-time managers know what it really takes to lead, to earn the trust and respect of your team, to develop a culture that leads to high performance, or to communicate in a way that moves people.

Being promoted up the ranks is exciting, but unfortunately, the typical organization does an underwhelming job of preparing its new managers for success. There is no single handbook on how to go from being responsible for your own success to being responsible for the success of many. As a result, the first promotion you land, moving from team member to team leader, will be the toughest transition of them all. There are few directions that prepare you for the surprising roles you will play for your team. There aren't many guides that will show you how to navigate the tricky social dynamics of being a good coach to people who previously saw you as a peer. I hope this book fills that gap.

BECOMING THE LEARNING LEADER

I believe that every person has the ability to lead. It's just a matter of learning how.

For me, that meant pursuing my master's degree in business in the hope that it would help me improve as a manager. While I'm glad I earned my MBA, I didn't entirely enjoy the experience. It was too restrictive, and the classes didn't cover topics I needed to know at a deep level. I wanted to learn directly from the people who fascinated me the most.

As fate would have it, the serendipity of a seat assignment for a flight to Lake Tahoe in 2014 set me on the unexpected path of doing just that. As I sat down and stretched my legs in my exit row seat, I found myself next to a friend of Todd Wagner. Todd Wagner founded Broadcast.com and eventually sold it to Yahoo! for billions. He did this with his partner, future investment "shark" and Dallas Mavericks owner Mark Cuban.

Over the course of this flight out west, I told my new friend about my desire to learn more and to create my own cast of teachers in the form of people who have lived lives of excellent leadership. By the time we landed, he had agreed to connect me with someone on Todd's team. Soon after, I met Todd for dinner.

Todd arrived about an hour early at the hotel where we were going to have dinner, and I was fortunate to spend this time with the self-made billionaire at the bar.

He was as kind as he was wise. I was blown away by his intelligence and his humble nature. I peppered him with questions. I wanted to learn about the what, who, why, and how at Broadcast.com. I was eager to hear how they looked the leaders of Yahoo! in the eye and said, "Look, you're either going to buy us or you'll have to compete with us. You decide." Todd and Mark concluded their meeting and walked away with $5.7 billion.

It was an incredible story, but I had one regret. I wished I had recorded the conversation. I wanted to pass along what I had learned to others. That dinner gave me a taste of what I could learn if I went directly to the source of the knowledge I so badly wanted to gain. In fact, I started thinking about how to have more conversations like that one—and how to share them with others. Through that confluence of events, I decided to create an interview-format podcast as my own virtual PhD program and call it *The Learning Leader Show*. By doing this, I would not only give influential leaders a reason to sit down for a conversation with me, I would also be able to share it and serve others in their leadership journey.

This is also why I've written this book. I understand your pain and dilemmas. I was there, too. I made countless mistakes during my years as a first-time manager, so in this book, I've taken everything I've learned from my own experience, research, and interviews with over 300 of the brightest leadership minds in the world, and I'm sharing it with you. I've distilled hard-won wisdom from my messy experiences and those of others I've learned from in order to make it easier and faster for you to become an excellent leader.

This book is for and about you. Many of you have worked for a bad boss (as have I). I care deeply about great leadership and recognize that it is exceedingly rare. The leaders in our lives have broad influence. When you earn a role as a new leader, my hope is that this book helps you use your power for good. My goal is to help accelerate your leadership education. I want you to be better able to make great decisions and to avoid some of the mistakes that I made as a first-time manager. Bad leadership is a costly epidemic. This book is part of my contribution to help eradicate that in whatever way I can. I want your contribution to the world of leadership to be a long-lasting net positive.

Here's how I've structured the book:

Part I: Lead Yourself. I very much believe in the mantra "You can't lead anyone without first leading yourself." So before we get to how to lead others, we will start with you—how you learn, what you learn, who you learn from, and why it's so important to continue learning throughout your life. We will explore the challenges of leading yourself both inside and out, and examine the tools and tactics for overcoming any and all obstacles.

Part II: Build Your Team. Before the roster of an effective team can be assembled, the idea of what makes for an effective team must be established. That means building a healthy team culture, and Part II will start there. With an understanding of culture in place, we will then move to the nuts and bolts of building the roster through hiring (and firing), as well as developing trust and earning respect.

Part III: Lead Your Team. Finally, we will discuss how to succeed at doing what managers *actually do*: setting a clear strategy and vision for your team, communicating them (and a myriad of other things) effectively, and ultimately driving the results everyone is counting on your team to deliver.

Throughout the book you will find helpful mental models, templates, key takeaways, insights, and advice from some of the most forward-thinking leaders around the world. Through case studies, research, personal stories, and the messages of the many leaders I've interviewed, this book will provide every new leader with the guidance needed for this important step in your career.

This is the book I wish I had when I was first promoted to a management role. I hope it will help you make the leap from individual contributor to manager with greater ease, grace, courage, and effectiveness.

PART I

LEAD YOURSELF

Augult afternoons in Green Bay, Wisconsin, are surprisingly hot, humid affairs. Every year, thousands of people spend those sticky days around a carefully constructed chain-link fence, with one goal: watching their beloved Packers prepare for the upcoming season. Within the fence, the players and coaching staff are focused on the work of training camp.

My younger brother, AJ, played nine seasons for the Packers. During every year of AJ's time in Green Bay, my dad spent the week of his birthday attending these August training camp practices. Most fans make the effort to arrive early at Ray Nitschke Field (located next to the Don Hutson Center and across the street from Lambeau Field) in order to get a good seat for the entertaining full team scrimmage near the end of the practice.

Not my dad; he always arrived early for another reason. He was fascinated by the first 45 minutes of the afternoon sessions, what is called a "walk through." At the beginning of *every* practice, these big, fast, incredibly strong, world-class athletes spend 45 minutes rehearsing their techniques and fundamentals. They focus on the smallest details every single day, and they do it *individually*. Why? Because before anyone is ready to practice performing as a team, they must make sure each of them is dialed in. And no player, regardless of who they are, is exempt from this preparatory requirement. AJ was a two-time All-American, won the Lombardi Award as the nation's top linebacker in college, and was the Packers' first round draft pick (number five overall) in 2006. And yet, every day in August, at the start of every practice, there he was working on the tiniest details of the techniques of his position, just like the lowliest undrafted rookie, just like Aaron Rodgers—another Packers first round draft pick, two-time NFL MVP, and one of the greatest quarterbacks of all time.

For AJ, the seemingly monotonous work was invaluable: "It's about the tiny details consistently worked on every day, so they become instincts. In the moment, you don't have to think; you can just rely on the instincts you created." And for that one week every August, there my dad would be, standing in the Wisconsin sun by that chain-link fence, loving every boring minute of it.

I share that story here at the start because it illustrates a fundamental principle about leadership and performance that I believe in down to my core, and that is this: you can't lead anyone else successfully over the long term until you take ownership of leading yourself. This is why before we start looking at how to manage your new responsibilities as a leader, we must begin with focusing on you.

If you are like I was when I got that first promotion to management, it may be tempting to skip this section entirely and jump to Parts II and III. You may be saying to yourself, "Lead myself? I can come back to this part another time. Right now, I need to know how to get a handle on the job I now find myself in!" As a question, it is understandable . . . but also shortsighted and misguided.

There are two foundational reasons why focusing on leading yourself well is the proper starting point to learning how to lead others:

Building skills. Having the qualifications necessary to get that new management job is not the same as having the skills to *do* the job of leading others. You are about to discover that issues you thought were obviously black and white as an employee are now shrouded in shades of gray as a manager, and the skills that made you an excellent performer in your previous role are quite different from those required for your new responsibility—getting *others* to be excellent performers. In order to develop these skills, refine them, and keep them honed and relevant, you are going to have to embrace the mindset, attitudes, behaviors, and habits of a self-driven learner.

Earning credibility. Do not expect respect, buy-in, and attentiveness from your team as an automatic benefit of your new role and title as their boss. *Compliance can be commanded, but commitment cannot.* People reserve their full capacity for emotional commitment for leaders they find credible, and credibility must be earned. Whether on the field or in the office, the best way to go about earning the credibility that leads to commitment is by modeling the behaviors you want your team to exhibit.

Let's turn our attention to the next two chapters, which focus on the single most important person you are responsible for leading well: *you.*

1

LEAD YOURSELF ON THE INSIDE

You can't influence unless you are willing to be influenced.
—JIM TRESSEL
President, Youngstown State University
(Episode #62, *The Learning Leader Show*)

THE STARTING POINT: SELF-AWARENESS

As listeners of my podcast, *The Learning Leader Show* (www.Learning Leader.com), know, every leader in conversation with me is likely to hear some variation of this question: *What are the commonalities of those who sustain excellence over an extended period of time?* After hundreds of responses from some of the most accomplished people in the world, I am struck by a common thread that runs through nearly every one of them: they all point to the person staring at you in the mirror. The best leaders all know that leading yourself well is step one to leading anyone else successfully.

To do that, we must begin by taking a hard look at what is happening in your heart and mind. The real work of leadership begins inside your own head.

To move the world, we must first move ourselves.
—SOCRATES

But *how* do you do this? What does it mean to "lead oneself well on the inside"? Before you can start the work of improving something, first, you must have taken stock of the relevant facts in play about that something. When it comes to your finances, that means starting with the basic step of measuring and tracking where your money is invested. Personal finance advisor Ramit Sethi wrote a book about it called *I Will Teach You to Be Rich*. When it comes to warfare, that means knowing the terrain, the enemy's forces, and your own. Ancient Chinese military strategist Sun Tzu wrote a book about it called *The Art of War*. When it comes to leading yourself, that means embracing the work of studying yourself, which leads to self-awareness. And yes, there's an expert with a book about that, too. Her name is Tasha Eurich, and the book is *Insight*.

According to Eurich, self-awareness is more than understanding just a single perspective of ourselves. Instead, it encompasses two aspects that are different but connected, like two sides of the same coin. In a recent *Harvard Business Review* article, she outlined the two broad categories of self-awareness:

> Self-awareness isn't one truth. It's a delicate balance of two distinct, even competing, viewpoints. . . . The first, which we dubbed *internal self-awareness*, represents how clearly we see our own values, passions, aspirations, fit with our environment, reactions (including thoughts, feelings, behaviors, strengths, and weaknesses), and impact on others. . . . The second category, *external self-awareness*, means understanding how other people view us, in terms of those same factors listed above.[1]

When I interviewed Eurich about her work, she shared a finding from her research that really caught my attention. Over the course of 10 studies involving nearly 5,000 participants, Eurich's team found that "95 percent of people think that they're self-aware but only 10 to 15 percent of people actually are. So the joke I always make is that on a good day 80 percent of us are lying to ourselves about whether we're lying to ourselves."[2] Think about that for a second. The biggest obstacle to developing self-awareness is the mistaken belief that you already possess self-awareness!

To overcome the blinders of faux self-awareness, Eurich prescribes a regular habit of questions aimed inward that target your own assumptions. "What I learned from studying people who have made these really dramatic improvements and transformations in their level of self-knowledge is that they work at it every day. It's a daily, incremental commitment. . . . It's about collecting and gathering those daily insights so that you can tie it up together and see the progress you've made over time."[3]

Author Geoff Colvin agrees. "The best performers observe themselves closely. They are in effect able to step outside themselves, monitor what is happening in their own minds, and ask how it's going. Researchers call this metacognition—knowledge about your own knowledge, thinking about your own thinking. Top performers do this much more systematically than others do; it's an established part of their routine."[4]

Let me explain the foundational role of self-awareness to success by way of an analogy. When I think of the duality of self-awareness and the constant posture of observation required to nurture it, I can't help but equate it to the mental asset every quarterback must possess to succeed in the game of football at any level: pocket awareness.

If you're not familiar with the term, pocket awareness refers to a quarterback's sense of what's going on around him as the defensive rushers close in, even as he maintains his focus downfield, looking for an open receiver to throw to. Like self-awareness, pocket awareness is a multidimensional sense of observing, tracking, understanding, and adjusting. A quarterback's awareness needs to be focused inside the pocket, where he must constantly be aware of:

- His footwork amid the shape-shifting mass of humanity around him
- His ability to find a throwing lane through the human picket fence of blockers and defenders

- The rushing defensive lineman, scraping linebacker, or blitzing safety who is coming in fast to take him to the ground with as much malice and force as the rules will allow

At the same time a quarterback's mind is monitoring what's happening *inside* the pocket, there's also the matter of what's going on *outside* the pocket. The quarterback can't use his eyes to see what is happening with the rush in the pocket because he must keep his gaze aimed downfield, watching to see how the rest of the defense is reacting to the play as it unfolds. He must keep a mental map of where his receivers are going to be and a running clock of when they will be there, all without actually watching them move. If the quarterback forgets this and stares at the receiver he wants to throw to, the defensive backs will simply follow his gaze to the spot where an interception is likely.

If the defense succeeds in collapsing the pocket and the quarterback is forced to flee, his awareness must factor in new variables—whether he should try to run to move the ball upfield, or simply to buy time to find a place to throw. If he chooses to do the latter, the quarterback must also keep a portion of his mind holding onto a model of where the line of scrimmage is and be able to *feel* when he must throw the ball just prior to crossing it.

Set aside the fact that this whole sequence typically occurs in three seconds or less, or that it involves very real physical danger every play. Instead, focus on this fact: if the quarterback ceases to have a factual, honest awareness of any one of those variables, the play will be a failure. When those failures start to pile up, and busted plays with negative outcomes outnumber the successful, positive plays, then the quarterback has failed his team as its leader. It's harsh, but it's true.

So it is with you as the leader of your team and your own self-awareness. If you don't have a clear *internal* understanding of who you are—both your strengths and your weaknesses—as well as a realistic *external* picture of how others perceive you, then the plays you try to get your team to run will also fail. You may miss an opportunity to leverage a strength in a more impactful way. Or you may continue to act out the script of morale-killing character flaws that lie hidden in your blind spots. Even when you do have a good grasp of your own stuff, if you don't really know how others perceive you, your messages and efforts to stir group effort will fall flat. Simply put: a leader who lacks a well-developed sense of both aspects of self-awareness is a leadership failure waiting to happen.

Now, to be totally honest, I wasn't always the kind of leader who would have passed that test. Growing up, I wasn't interested in learning about myself in this way. I was focused on hard work and doing whatever my coaches told me to do to become the best I could be, but I certainly didn't make a habit of seeking feedback from others.

That has certainly changed over time. As I grew up, my experiences changed from leading my team of buddies onto the field to leading my team of employees toward the performance goals handed to us by our company. The more life experience I got and the more I learned from reading (and learning from great mentors), the more I realized how little I knew. From that first seed of insight a tree of self-awareness has grown within me. I share this to say: self-awareness is not something that you either have or you don't. It is something that can be pursued, built, and grown all in one. If I could do it, so can you.

Self-awareness comes over time and with practice. A great place to start is by making use of self-assessment surveys and coaching relationships to help you understand yourself on a deeper level. There is great value in taking self-assessment tests. They give you the opportunity to see yourself through a different lens. Some good options to assess your personality type include the Hogan Personality Inventory,[5] the Hexaco Personality Inventory,[6] or the *Strengths Finder 2.0* from Gallup and Tom Rath.[7]

Of course, each of these tests has a limit to the benefits they provide. They rely on assumptions that place people into one category or another, when in fact individuals typically fall into a spectrum of behavior that changes based on their mindset and setting.[8] You might test in one category one day, only to retest and find yourself in a different category because your circumstances have changed. As with everything else about developing and sustaining self-awareness, personality inventories are not "the answer." They are just one data point in a long line of continuous inquiry.

THE ROLE OF CURIOSITY

Curiosity refers to an appetite for learning and the hunger to understand. Psychology researchers Todd Kashdan of George Mason University and Paul Silvia of the University of North Carolina at Greensboro define curiosity as "the recognition, pursuit, and intense desire to explore novel, challenging, and uncertain events."[9] When we are curious, "we are fully aware and receptive to whatever exists and might happen in the present moment," and are motivated "to act and think in new ways and investigate, be immersed, and learn about whatever is the immediate interesting target of [our] attention."[10]

Curiosity is about more than just having an inquisitive nature. As research has shown, curiosity serves as an amplifier of one's natural intellectual capacity, as recognized by more quantitative measures like IQ. According to work done in the Fullerton Longitudinal Study, a 30-year study of the development of giftedness by researchers at California State University, researchers found:

> Those gifted with curiosity are gifted in their own right. Students with gifted curiosity outperformed their peers on a wide range of educational outcomes, including math and reading, SAT scores, and college attainment. According to ratings from teachers, the motivationally gifted students worked harder and learned more.[11]

There is a vast difference between those who approach the world with a genuine intellectual curiosity and those who don't, and it can be summed up in one word: *growth*. Curious people are growing people. As you embark on your journey of transition from being responsible for your own performance to being responsible for the performance of others, you are going to have to grow in a variety of ways. Cultivating a mindset of curiosity is the best way I know of to jump-start that process of learning and growth.

Think of curiosity as a high-octane fuel. For that fuel to burn productively, you need an engine to pour it into that can transform its power into momentum. You'll need to build a machine in your mind.

BUILDING YOUR LEARNING MACHINE

What are the commonalities of those who sustain excellence over an extended period of time? These six words: build yourself into a learning machine. The concept of becoming a *learning machine* was made popular by Charlie Munger, one of the titans behind the investment firm Berkshire Hathaway. In his commencement address to the graduates of the University of Southern California Gould School of Law in 2007, Munger explained the secret to the success enjoyed by Warren Buffett and Berkshire Hathaway:

> If you take Berkshire Hathaway, which is certainly one of the best regarded corporations in the world and may have the best long-term investment record in the entire history of civilization, the skill that got them through one decade would not have sufficed to get it through the next decade with the achievements made. Without Warren Buffett being a learning machine, a continuous learning machine, the record would have been absolutely impossible.
>
> The same is true at lower walks of life. I constantly see people rise in life who are not the smartest, sometimes not even the most diligent, but they are learning machines, they go to bed every night a little wiser than when they got up and boy does that help particularly when you have a long run ahead of you.[12]

I love it because "learning machine" efficiently captures two important concepts: thoughtfulness and intentionality. If someone were to throw my question back at me, these two ideas would be my answer. Surveying the landscape of conversations I have had with high-performing leaders of all kinds, these are the commonalities that I see among them as they pursue consistent excellence. They are deeply thoughtful in their approach and supremely intentional in their effort. As these leaders encounter experiences (whether successful or unsuccessful ones), they have a process in place to reflect, think, analyze what happened, and (most important) grow from the experience. They are intentional about what they do, why they do it, how they do it, and with whom they do it—thoughtfulness and intentionality are the twin pistons that drive the internal combustion engine of successful leading. This is the image I think of when I hear Charlie Munger talk about being a "learning machine."

Learning hard things is an active exercise of thought. It is not simply a process of downloading information into our brains. When we have new ideas, perspectives, or experiences, our thoughtful contemplation of what they are, why they exist, and what to do with them is how learning happens. When you read a book, do you take notes and analyze what you learned? When you have an interaction with a colleague, do you think about why it went well and how it could have gone better?

While it is certainly possible to learn passively, this isn't optimal. Passive learners have a low ceiling on their learning potential, whereas those who approach learning with purpose, focus, and effort do far better. If thoughtfulness is the instrument of learning, intentionality is the power.

A person who is a "learning machine" is intentionally and constantly seeking new information with the goal of becoming better. Machines are not organic; they don't spontaneously generate. They have to be built. And, increasingly in our modern digital age, they also must be programmed. The same is true for a person to become a learning machine.

Like the interest that accrues over time in the long-term style of investing that Warren Buffet advocates, the benefits of building yourself into an engine of learning compound. It doesn't matter what set of skills and deficiencies you bring to a job, an assignment, or a moment of adversity. What you have at the start won't define how it ends because by being in constant learning mode you evolve throughout the process.

A great example comes from the American Civil War. In *The Leadership Moment,* Michael Useem, professor of management at Wharton, tells the story of Joshua Lawrence Chamberlain, a college professor from Maine, who had no military training when he volunteered to join the Union Army.[13] At the time he signed up, he is reported to have told the governor of Maine, "I have always been interested in military matters, and what I do not know in that line, I can learn. I study, I tell you, every military work I can find."[14]

By the time the war came to the Pennsylvania town of Gettysburg, then Colonel Chamberlain had been put in command of the 20th Maine Volunteer Infantry Regiment. During the bloodiest battle of the war, Chamberlain made a tactical decision for which he has been credited with saving Major General George Meade's Army of the Potomac, turning the tide, and setting the Confederacy on the path to defeat. While protecting a small hill now known as Little Round Top, Chamberlain's regiment found itself without ammunition as it faced an attack. Instead of retreating and giving up the defense of the Union Army's left flank, Chamberlain made the quick decision to lead one of the most famous counterattacks in history. Calling on his men to affix bayonets to their otherwise useless rifles, he led the men of the 20th Maine on a downhill charge into the lines of Confederate soldiers of the 15th Alabama Regiment, capturing many rebel soldiers and sending the rest into retreat.

Despite having had no formal military training, Chamberlain's snap decision was the product of a life spent as a self-driven learner. Prior to ever joining the army at the outbreak of the war, Chamberlain had read every book he could find on military strategy, most notably studying the work of Napoleon Bonaparte. Once in the army, Chamberlain requested to be the tent mate of Adelbert Ames, who had trained at West Point.[15] As Chamberlain later told it, "I asked him [Ames] every night to tell me what he knew so I could learn."

Joe Navarro is another great example. When Joe was a young child, his family came to the United States as refugees fleeing the communist revolutionaries that took over Cuba. As the family settled into their unexpected new life as immigrants in Miami, Joe could not speak a word of English. Through intentional observation and focus, Joe learned to read the body language of the English-speaking adults around him. He continued to study the signals of nonverbal communication even after learning to speak the language of his new home.

> In the 1970s, there weren't many books on body language. There were probably one or two. There weren't even courses at the university. I enjoyed and pursued it because it was fascinating to me. You could go from one country to another and experience very similar behaviors. So I started reading the great masters—Darwin, who had written about body language, comparing it to the animals, the work of Edward Hall and others. It wasn't my major in college. It wasn't something that was being offered, but it certainly was something that I enjoyed studying on my own. It was something that I focused on.[16]

Because of this intentional, thoughtful approach to learning something—first out of necessity, and then out of interest—Joe was recruited to join the Federal Bureau of Investigation, where he put his knowledge to work catching criminals and spies over the course of a 25-year FBI career. He is now an internationally bestselling author and recognized as one of the world's premier experts on nonverbal communication and body language assessment.

That is the power of building yourself into a learning machine.

THE CYCLE OF LEARNING: THE OPERATING FRAMEWORK

Of course, before any machine can be built successfully, first, it must be designed. Blueprints come before the cement can be poured for buildings and bridges, CAD drawings come before the metal can be stamped for cars, and plans come before they can be executed. Building yourself into a learning machine is no different.

Because I believe deeply in the value of learning, I have taken the time to think about *how* I learn the best. I recognized that learning happens most often and most effectively for me when it is part of a continuous process. Once I identified that process, I took the next step and *wrote it down*. The blueprint is shown in the following figure. This is a framework to operationalize my learning. Without it, I end up doing what education expert and classroom teacher Jackie Gerstein calls "leaving learning up to chance."[17]

It's not what you know that counts. It's how fast you can learn, because what you know is going to be way in the rearview mirror. And I think that the discipline that we need right now is this rapid cycle learning.

—LIZ WISEMAN
Bestselling author of *Rookie Smarts* and *Multipliers* and CEO of The Wiseman Group
(Episode #160, *The Learning Leader Show*)

Let's dive into each of the four steps in this cycle in more detail.

Step One: Learn

The beginning of any learning cycle starts with the intake of information. Taking charge of this process means proactively seeking information from people you trust and from those who have been where you want to go. There is no substitute for reliable expertise and the wisdom of experience. I source my learning from three categories: mentors, virtual mentors, and coaches.

Mentors

These are people who have done what I want to do or have attained the position that I want to attain. Mentors are usually able to look at where you are in your career and offer specific guidance about how to move forward. Some mentors are built into your life (like your parents, for example), while others you will have to seek out. The best mentors are those with whom you can build a real relationship. This is critical because the most important role a mentor fills is that of being the source of direct, honest feedback to help you improve. That kind of vulnerability and risk doesn't thrive in a pairing dictated by a boss or HR as part of a company-administered mentoring program. In order to get to the deep value that a mentor can provide, you have to know the person is trustworthy and truly cares about you and your improvement. (The same is true for the mentor as well. The bond of a genuine relationship enables mentors to put in the emotional work of thinking deeply about you and taking the risk of telling you what you need to hear but may not want to hear.)

Kim Malone Scott, author of the *New York Times* and *Wall Street Journal* bestselling book *Radical Candor*, identifies the prerequisite for a mentor or boss to be able to successfully deliver challenging feedback to a mentee or employee: they must genuinely care for the person to whom they are delivering the hard truth. When Kim was leading the AdSense business at Google, she reported to Sheryl Sandberg. After delivering a presentation on how the business was doing to then CEO Eric Schmidt and founder Sergey Brin, Kim's confidence was soaring. They had recognized the value of her team's work and had peppered her with the kinds of questions anybody in her position would've wanted to hear: "What do you need? More engineering resources? More marketing budget?"

"Why don't you walk back to my office with me?" Sheryl told Kim as they left the meeting. As anyone who has ever had a boss ask that question knows, Kim's mind immediately went into overdrive: "Oh boy, I screwed something up. I have no idea what it is, but I'm sure I'm about to hear about it." After Sheryl began with the list of positive things that Kim had done in the meeting, she transitioned to the reason she had called this post-meeting debrief.

"You said 'um' a lot in there. Do you realize that?"

In Kim's words to me, she "breathed a huge sigh of relief. If that was all I had done wrong, it didn't really matter. I was fine. I kind of did a brush-off gesture with my hand and said, 'Yeah, I know. It's a verbal tic. No big deal really.'"

Sheryl didn't waver. She went on, "I know a really good speech coach. Would you like an introduction?"

Once again, Kim repeated the brush-off gesture. "No, I'm busy. Didn't you hear about those new customers?"

Sheryl stopped, looked Kim directly in the eye, and delivered the kind of brutal truth that can only be safely delivered within the boundaries of a caring relationship.

"When you say 'um' every third word, it makes you sound stupid."
As Kim told me,

> Now she has my full attention. Some people would say it was
> mean of Sheryl to say that I sounded stupid, but it was the kind-
> est thing she could have possibly done for me in that moment of
> my career. She wouldn't have said it that way to anyone else on
> her team because everyone else were better listeners than me and
> weren't quite as bullheaded. But she knew those were the kind
> of words she had to say to get through to me in order to get me
> to see the speaking coach. And when I went to that coach, I had
> the painful experience of watching myself give a speech. I learned
> something important. Sheryl wasn't exaggerating. I really did say
> "um" every third word, and this was news to me. I had been giv-
> ing presentations my entire career. I had raised $35 million giving
> presentations. I thought I was pretty good at it.
> This got me to thinking, *Why had nobody else told me?*
> It was like I was walking through my career with my fly down
> and nobody had the common courtesy to tell me. So, why had
> nobody told me, and what made it so seemingly easy for Sheryl
> to tell me? . . . Caring personally: I knew Sheryl cared about me
> as a human being. . . . Because she had [my] growth in mind, she
> wasn't going to pull her punches when [I] screwed up. She was
> willing to challenge [me] very directly.[18]

Brent Beshore, the CEO of private equity investment firm
adventur.es, says that a key ingredient of the people that you look to for
mentoring and guidance is that they need to be "rooting for you." As he
told me during my interview with him, "I try to surround myself with
people who will tell me the truth, and who I give an open invitation to
be honest with me, even when I don't want to hear the truth. . . . Any-
time somebody is providing criticism, it should always be constructive,
and it should always be loving, kind, and gentle."[19] That last point is very
important. If the people who are advising you aren't truly rooting for

your success, then their guidance could be colored by ulterior motives, and those types of people are not helpful.

Beyond someone who genuinely cares about you, look for mentors who help you think about solving problems, who will ask you questions, and help *you* come to a solution. When you ask them for advice, these types of mentors will typically say, "I don't have enough information to answer that question, but here is what I would think about to solve those problems. . . ."

As with any relationship, the exchange of value should be mutual. Whatever one calls it, it's not a relationship if one person is always giving, and the other is always taking. But that can create a quandary. Often, a younger, inexperienced person will email me, asking, "How can I add value to my mentor? I don't have anything to offer." Yes, you do! Everyone does. Here is an example of an easy way to bring what you have to the table and provide real value to your mentor every time you meet.

After each meeting with your mentor, thank them and write a detailed follow-up with everything you learned and how you will implement it in your life. Then suggest that your mentor forward your email to anyone else they mentor. This does several things for the mentor:

1. It shows that you are a good listener.
2. It shows you are diligent, that you took notes, and that you care.
3. It shows that you think about unique ways to help other people.
4. It adds value to their life.

A great mentor often doesn't take time to document their thoughts on specific topics. *You can do this for them.* This will differentiate you from 99 percent of the population, and your mentor will be grateful for it.

One last point about mentors. They are most definitely not just for the younger, inexperienced person. I recently had the privilege of getting to sit down and record a conversation in person with the legendary basketball figure George Raveling. Despite being supremely accomplished, George floored me when he told me about the mentors he continues to seek out at the age of 81 years. After reading Ryan

Holiday's book *The Obstacle Is the Way*, George jumped at the chance to meet Ryan when a mutual friend offered to make the introduction. About his relationship with Ryan, George told me:

> I don't know anybody in the last 10 years who's had more of an impact on my life than him. The people he introduces me to, the things he's taught me. He's been part of a change in my mentality that I realized. When you're 81 years old, you need four or five young mentors. Young people in your life that can help you understand and navigate through the twenty-first century. You have to have four or five mentors who are young, who can teach you, and whom you trust. You have to have the willingness to be vulnerable to the way they think. I have four or five of those people that could be my sons, but they are all my teachers. They are my mentors. I listen to them. I ask them questions. I ask, "How would you handle this?" I need a young person's perspective. I would say to all of those modern elders out there: if you really want to accelerate your growth, get four young dudes and let them be your mentors.[20]

Virtual Mentors

Virtual mentors are people you may never meet, but who teach you from afar. Books are one of the greatest ways to learn from experts from all over the world. Anyone can invest $15 and get the treasured secrets of the brightest minds on the planet. How great is that? I can see into the mind of Marcus Aurelius for practically nothing by reading *Meditations*. Management guru and excellence evangelist Tom Peters has shared everything he's learned in his latest book, *The Excellence Dividend*. His life's wisdom will cost you a total of $17. I know the behind-the-scenes story of how Phil Knight built Nike because he took the time to document everything in his book, *Shoe Dog*. Gretchen Rubin gave me new insights into my personality through her book, *The Four Tendencies*.

Charlie Munger, whom I discussed earlier, said with beautiful simplicity: "In my whole life, I have known no wise people who didn't read all the time. None, zero."[21] With the success Charlie has had and the people he has encountered over his 95 years of life, that is saying something.

Don't believe you have time to read a book? I'm willing to bet you have more time available than you think. It doesn't take hours of nightly reading to benefit from the power of having a great author serve as your virtual mentor. Life and growth are all about the accumulation of tiny bits of progress (more on that later). Start with just 15 minutes each night. Intentionally turn off the TV, power-down your work computer, set aside your phone, and pick up a book. You will be surprised at how many great books you can get through if you consistently read each day, even if only for 15 minutes a night. And you will sleep better, too. Research has shown that reading as little as *six minutes* can reduce stress levels by up to 68 percent, outperforming other relaxation techniques like listening to music (61 percent).[22]

But let's assume that even 15 minutes before bed isn't doable. Then that is where the power of audiobooks and podcasts come in. Whether it is during your daily commute to and from work or while you are logging miles doing your exercise of choice, there are plenty of opportunities to *listen* to the wisdom of others while keeping your hands and eyes free to do something else.

Thanks to the power of fiber optics, cellular communications, and ubiquitous Wi-Fi access, you can watch videos of your virtual mentors wherever you are, whether on your desktop, laptop, or on your phone. From TED Talks and similarly styled video content on platforms such as YouTube and Vimeo to the content feeds of users on Facebook and LinkedIn, we can access some of the best and brightest speakers of our generation at the click of a button. In just 20 minutes, we can learn about some of the most cutting-edge ideas transforming life on our planet today.

Wherever you get your information, it's important to be selective about the knowledge you take in. Prior to reading a book, I look closely at who made the recommendation and *why* they thought it was useful. Then I'll study the author. What have they done? How have they mastered the topic? I know Kim Scott is one of the best teachers in the world on how to be a radically candid boss because she did the work for many years. And she worked for some of the brightest leadership minds in the world. I know Charlie McMahan understands how to build a tribe from less than 50 people to more than 5,000 strong because he's spent 25 years *doing it* and learning from others along the way. I know Maria Taylor understands what it takes to quickly ascend the career ladder because she's doing it *right now* and has surrounded herself with a world-class mentor team. I know Bill Curry understands what it means to be a champion because he won championships playing for one of the greatest football coaches of all time, Vince Lombardi. Additionally, he's taken what he learned from his great coaches and teammates and taught others for over 50 years.

Coaches

As a quarterback, I experienced the value of great coaching. When I was led by an exceptional coach, I played better than when I had an average coach. But why do people tend to think of coaching as only belonging in the world of competition, whether in sports or otherwise? Coaching isn't about competition; it is about *skill development.* No matter the domain, if you are aiming to improve yourself by developing a skill, you need someone who understands that skill to be on your sideline, wearing the coach's hat.

I've made it a personal habit to seek out people who can give me specific feedback, who can draw from a base of expertise that makes it feedback worth getting. For instance, when it comes to improving my skills as a speaker and a writer, I have a handpicked coach whom I trust to give it to me straight. Prior to us working together as colleagues in the corporate world, Lance Salyers honed his writing chops and public speaking skills in the courtroom as a prosecuting attorney.

During his decade plus arguing cases before judges and juries, Lance handled high-profile and complex cases to award-winning acclaim. The Association of Government Attorneys in Capital Litigation awarded Lance their Trial Advocacy Award for his work prosecuting a Cincinnati man for the murder of his girlfriend (who was also his attorney) and then of a witness.[23] The Investigation Discovery channel featured another one of Lance's trials: a complex case against twin brothers who were both pediatricians, and who were both sexually abusing their young male patients for decades, using prescription drugs and piles of money to buy their victims' silence.[24] Once he moved to the corporate world, I saw how Lance's courtroom experience made for entertaining and compelling presentations that were entirely unique in our business environment.

I share this information about Lance's background to make a larger point about coaches in general. I know if I want to sharpen my skills at building a message, supporting it with both sound evidence and compelling stories, and delivering it in an entertaining, persuasive, and attention-holding way, Lance can give me both the high-level perspective and ground-level tweaks to help me do that. It doesn't matter that he doesn't check the traditional boxes for a speaking coach. What matters is his demonstrated skill in both the realm of public speaking and—equally important—the ability to translate his skill into teachable insights that I can understand and apply.

What Kim Scott said about Sheryl Sandberg and mentors is equally applicable to coaches. Because Lance and I are both former colleagues and friends, I know he genuinely cares about me and my development as a communicator. The importance of this can't be overstated. The best coaches are not just dispensers of expertise and corrective suggestions; they are the ones who are rooting for you to succeed. When Lance gives the sharp critique of an expert, it's easier to absorb and apply—even though it can sting—because I know he wants to see me become the best I can be. That's what coaching is all about, and it is invaluable.

People often use "mentor" and "coach" interchangeably. Both are necessary to maximize our knowledge and skills, but they are not the same.

A mentor is someone who provides guidance, who listens to your experiences and responds with insight. A mentor can help you lay out plans to chart your future path, plans that might include hiring a coach. A coach has a much more defined role.

A coach works to actively develop your knowledge and skills to perform. A coach gives specific assignments for you to take in new information. A coach designs drills and experiences, a purposeful practice aimed at developing skills particular to your work. Perhaps the most important role a coach plays is providing task-specific feedback after observing your efforts in a performance area. We engage coaches in multiple aspects of our lives—to help us lose weight, to teach us to play guitar, to help us improve our golf game—to aid in our purposeful practice of a skill.

A mentor operates at a higher, strategic level, functioning more as a guide, while a coach focuses on the tactical details that will help drive us forward in our skill development program.

Not every person you engage with will be mentor or coach material, but every single engagement presents an opportunity to learn. Approaching each conversation with genuine curiosity can generate microlearning moments that can have a lasting impact on your life.

Step Two: Test

Whether you learn from a mentor or coach in person, or from a virtual mentor through a book or podcast, the information you've gathered won't do you any good if you don't take the next step: you must take action. It is only through the kinetic energy of putting ideas into use in your daily life that you can test your understanding of what you have learned and the value of that knowledge. As human performance coach Todd Herman put it to me, "The answers are never waiting for you while you're sitting at your desk trying to plan it out perfectly. Your answers lie on the field of play by getting out there and taking action."[25]

In his bestselling book *Outliers*, Malcolm Gladwell popularized the 10,000-hour rule, the idea that mastery of a skill required the investment of approximately 10,000 hours of time spent practicing that skill.[26] Turns out, that's only partially the case. Gladwell's rule of thumb is loosely based on research on expert performance done by Anders Ericsson, Conradi Eminent Scholar and professor of psychology at Florida State University. When I spoke with Ericsson, he made clear where Gladwell's popular take gets the science wrong:

> It's not just engaging in the domain, like the Beatles playing in front of audiences for thousands of hours. . . . In order to get better, you're actually going to have to do something to change how able you are to do something. We basically referred to that as "purposeful practice." . . . When you look at the scientific evidence, you really don't find that spending more time doing the same thing actually will improve your performance, when you measure it by objective criteria.[27]

In other words, it's not enough to simply practice. In order for the hours of practice to actually work, the practice must be accompanied by a feedback mechanism involving an expert. Ericsson outlined to me a four-step process for "deliberate practice":

1. Set a specific goal.
2. Cultivate intense focus.
3. Ask for immediate feedback.
4. Seek frequent discomfort.

Author Geoff Colvin puts it bluntly when he writes, "Deliberate practice is . . . highly demanding mentally, whether the activity is purely intellectual, such as chess or business-related activities, or heavily physical, such as sports; and it isn't much fun."[28]

Deliberate practice is "deep work," coupled with a coach to correct flaws and help make improvements. (We'll look into author Cal Newport's concept of "deep work" more closely in the next chapter.) Think of a golf pro standing by your side on the driving range as you practice hitting ball after ball after ball. As a manager, of course, your role is to be the person who provides the feedback for the people you lead. But you need to ensure you also have this mechanism in place, especially if your organization doesn't set this up for you. Who are the people in your life who can give you the kind of honest, useful feedback that turns regular action into deliberate practice?

Let me give you an example. Suppose you learn from a mentor (who is present) that the meetings you run with your team are disorganized and lacking a clear outcome. They are, in a word you can imagine your employees using, pointless. Upon hearing this, you quickly accept it as something you want to change. Accordingly, you set a goal: increase the efficiency and clarity of your meetings.

Then you start the work of preparing to accomplish that goal. You set aside time before your next team meeting to do some research, read up on different styles of communication, and set a clear strategy for yourself and for your meeting. In order to transform this implementation of your mentor's feedback about your meetings into a moment of deliberate practice, there's one more thing you should continue to do: have your mentor in your meetings. By taking this step, you build a feedback loop into the effort, enabling your mentor to deliver the performance judgments of a coach and new ideas to implement to get even better following the meeting.

Occasionally, you may find what you hear difficult to accept, particularly if you don't like the feedback and guidance that your mentor or coach gives you. This is where "frequent discomfort" comes in. The key is to remember that you *chose* your mentors and coaches. These aren't people with whom you are forced to engage; you selected them because of their wisdom and experience. Whenever I receive guidance that feels hard to take, I remind myself that I chose to get feedback from these people because they've done what I want to do. When viewed from that perspective, *their criticism is a gift.*

When I played football, we filmed not just every game, but every practice. From the time I was 14 years old, I reaped the benefits of this coaching feedback loop. Although it didn't feel good at first, over time I became comfortable watching my mistakes, taking feedback from coaches, and adjusting my play on the field. This is why I now make sure to have a videographer present as often as possible at my keynote speeches, so I can go over the film with my speaking coach. Investing in a feedback loop powered by genuine expertise has accelerated my learning into warp speed. In this vein, the input from your mentor or coach or boss isn't just a means of learning (Step One). Their feedback is an integral part of effective implementation and testing (Step Two).

Step Three: Reflect and Adjust

> *It is hard to learn from experience when we are*
> *not looking inward, at the true causes.*
> —ROBERT GREENE
> *The Laws of Human Nature*

Once you have taken the action that puts the new information you've learned into practice, it is tempting to move on immediately to the next new thing you can learn. Doing this short-circuits the process and skips a vital step: thoughtful reflection on the action you just took. Turning your learning and growth into an iterative cycle requires a look-back period. After the implementation work is done, set aside time to analyze your implementation efforts and ask yourself:

- "Did the steps I took based on the new information work?"
- "If so, *why?*" or
- "If not, *why not?*"

This is separate and distinct from the feedback loop of a coach or mentor in Step Two. There is something uniquely valuable about thoughtfully engaging in the process of evaluating our work *by ourselves.* Author and TED Talk phenom Susan Cain explained why it is so important to conduct some of the work of deliberate practice alone in her book, *Quiet: The Power of Introverts in a World That Can't Stop Talking.* "It takes intense concentration, and other people can be distracting. It requires deep motivation, often self-generated. But most important, it involves working on the task that's most challenging to you personally." Cain goes on to quote Anders Ericsson from her inter-view with him: "Only when you're alone, Ericsson told me, can you 'go directly to the part that's challenging you. If you want to improve what you're doing, you must be the one who generates the move. Imagine a group class—you're the one generating the move only a small percent-age of the time.'"

Educator and consultant Silvia Tolisano believes in the power of intentional reflection when it comes to learning. "Reflection is an important component of the learning process. It can NOT be seen as an add-on, something to be cut if time is running short. We have all heard John Dewey's quote: 'We don't learn from experience; we learn from reflecting on the experience.' . . . Asking a teacher to simply 'reflect' on a lesson taught or asking students to 'reflect' on their learn-ing, will often be met with blank stares. Being able to reflect is a skill learned, a habit to develop. Reflection requires metacognition (think-ing about your thinking), articulation of that thinking and the ability to make connections (past, present, future, outliers, relevant informa-tion, etc.)."[29] Achieving mental mastery is a conscious transformation gained through much study and purposeful practice.

Step Four: Teach

At some point on your travels on the Internet, you may have come across the ancient Chinese proverb attributed to Confucius: "I hear and I forget. I see and I remember. I do and I understand."[30] To that I would add "I teach and I know," based on the Latin phrase *docendo discimus* ("by teaching we learn").[31] This wisdom is no less true today than it was thousands of years ago. There is something unique about the power of teaching others that cements what you have learned.

Think about any moment that you were asked to give a presenta-tion. It could have been for an assignment back in school or a project given to you by your boss at work. Regardless of how well you ended up doing the actual presentation, the preparation you put in was a power-ful engine for learning to take place.

Interestingly, the studying done in preparation to teach is not the only reason teaching others solidifies learning *in the teacher*. After conducting a recent meta-analysis of over five dozen previously published research studies, researchers learned more about why the very act of speaking out loud the things you have learned is itself a key piece of the learning puzzle. This practice is known as self-explanation, and is defined as "a self-generated explanation of presented instruction that integrates the presented information with background knowledge and fills in tacit inferences."[32] According to the authors of a study published in the September 2018 issue of *Educational Psychology Review*, the tactic of self-explanation boosts learning and understanding more than other methods, such as note-taking, problem-solving work, and hearing the material explained to the learner.[33] This is true for both self-explanations that the learner spontaneously engages in as well as those prompted by the instructor. In either case, the act of self-explanation "'generate[s] inferences about causal connections and conceptual relationships that enhance understanding' . . . [while also helping] the learner reali[z]e what they don't know."[34] This act of explaining out loud to yourself what you are learning as a way of learning can also serve as a strategy for reading hard-to-understand material.[35]

Brett Brown, head coach of the NBA's Philadelphia 76ers, has incorporated this principle of teaching to learn into the cultural fabric of his team. On off-days during the season, Brown invites guest speakers to the team breakfast to deliver a talk to the team. The roster of guest speakers is quite varied, ranging from Hollywood film directors like M. Night Shyamalan to a person who spoke about the experience of being wrongfully convicted of a crime.[36] At least once each month, the invited speaker is neither a celebrity nor an outsider of any kind. On those mornings, one of the members of the team is tapped to deliver a talk, with the goal of teaching his teammates something about which he is interested. For center Amir Johnson, that meant talking about the history of tattoos. For forward Robert Covington, the topic was reptiles and featured an unexpected appearance by his pet, Max, a nearly four-foot-long bumblebee python.[37]

I love this story and have applied it to my *Learning Leader* circles (mastermind groups that I facilitate). I often ask circle members to prepare a "teaching" presentation on a topic of their choice. We discuss what it is and how they can best put a talk together based on what they've learned. When we finish, I have found they know significantly more about the topic of their choice (even after they already felt like they knew it well when they signed up for the assignment). My wife and I have incorporated this practice into our own lives. We have made it a habit to teach one another what we learn when either one of us reads a great book, listens to a helpful podcast, or watches an interesting documentary. The process of preparing to be "the teacher" enables greater absorption of the learned knowledge.

IT'S ALL ABOUT MINDSET

All of this internal, mental effort is designed to do one thing: to get you out from behind the walls of a fixed mindset and put you into the swift currents of a *growth mindset*. These terms come from Stanford psychologist Carol Dweck's seminal book, *Mindset: The New Psychology of Success*. It belongs on my personal Mt. Rushmore of books that have had a major impact on how I see the world and move through it. I highly recommend it. I want to close this chapter with a key insight she describes. Over the course of her work studying thousands of people—adults to children as young as preschoolers—a clear pattern emerged.

> Everyone is born with an intense drive to learn. Infants stretch their skills daily. . . . They never decide it's too hard or not worth the effort. . . . As soon as children become able to evaluate themselves, some of them become afraid of challenges. They become afraid of not being smart. . . . So children with the fixed mindset want to make sure they succeed. Smart people should always succeed. But for children with the growth mindset, success is about stretching themselves. It's about becoming smarter.[38]

What is true for children is also true for anyone in a leadership position. If you identify your success as having the right answers, then you will make choices aimed at protecting that image. We'll talk more about what that means for your team's culture in a later chapter, but this mindset will also have a devastating impact on *you*. Defining success as "being right" leads you to avoid tackling difficult challenges and hearing contrary information. In the end, this path will leave you no different than you were when you started on it. You will be no stronger, no smarter, and no more capable. As a result, you will be ill-equipped to face the big tasks your new position will inevitably demand of you. Don't let where you are now be the ceiling of your potential. Embrace the spirit of the mantra "Becoming is better than being."[39]

KEY INSIGHTS

- We must learn to lead ourselves before we can expect to effectively lead others.
- Build the skills to *do the job*, not to *get the job*.
- To earn credibility as a leader, we must model the desired behaviors for the group.
- The best performers cultivate a high level of self-awareness. They make this an established part of their routine.
- Become a learning machine. Your mode of operation is of a constant learner.
- Your curiosity is the high-octane fuel that propels your growth.
- Strengthened by a feedback-giving coach, purposeful practice leads to improvement. It can be difficult, sometimes frustrating work. Push through it.
- The highest-performing professionals in the world work on the tiniest details of the fundamentals of their craft every day.
- The framework for learning is intake/consume, test, reflect, and teach.
- Don't let your now become your ceiling. Becoming is better than being.

RECOMMENDED ACTIONS

- List and define the fundamentals of your job.
- Identify external resources that you will use to grow your knowledge and lead to growing your credibility as a leader.
- By teaching we learn. Create an opportunity to teach something at which you are not an expert. For example, take the lead on a project at work for which you'll present findings, or guest lecture at a local university.

2

LEAD YOURSELF
ON THE OUTSIDE

As the leader, you are the emotional thermostat for your team.
—Scott Belsky
EVP, Adobe, and Chief Product Officer, Creative Cloud
(Episode #276, *The Learning Leader Show*)

WHY SELF-DISCIPLINE MATTERS

It is hard to be disciplined. People who have discipline are able to do hard things. Why? Self-discipline gives them the ability to control their feelings and overcome their weaknesses, the ability to pursue what they think is right despite a multitude of temptations to abandon it. In the words of pioneering baseball mental skills coach Harvey Dorfman, it is through self-discipline that one "is a master of, rather than a slave to, his thoughts and emotions."[1] Therein lies the secret to turning all the intellectual learning we discussed in Chapter 1 into real, tangible change in the physical world. This process starts with mastering what we do with our bodies, with our time, with our effort.

Self-discipline is even more important in leadership because of the impact and effect people in positions of leadership have on those around them. Leading is lonely. Leading is hard. This is especially apparent as a new manager. By virtue of your new promotion, you will instantly become the topic of conversation of everyone who reports to you. They will closely watch what you do, what you say, how you say it, how you handle adversity, how you respond to success, how you prepare for a big moment with the CEO. In short, they will be watching your *every move*.

Notice I didn't say "the people *under* you." I point this out to make clear that the eyes that will be on you as a leader, studying what you do and how you do it, will belong to *more* than just the people you lead. Think about tossing a stone into a pond and creating ripples across the surface as a result. Being given a position of leadership is like being handed a larger rock. The ripples your actions make are larger, but note this obvious but important truth: *the ripples don't just travel in the direction you threw the stone.* No matter what your intended target audience, the ripples of your choices as a leader are seen by everyone around you.

This is why self-discipline matters.

As the leader of a team, you will be asking your team to do things that are hard. In order to make that ask with credibility, you must show a willingness to do hard things yourself. You must lead from the front. People follow leaders who they know will be there when it's hard.

WHAT SELF-DISCIPLINE LOOKS LIKE

Disciplined leaders seek out opportunities to test themselves by purposefully and aggressively seeking out discomfort. You can't know how far you can go without regularly putting yourself in situations where you are stretched beyond the known and the comfortable. One example of doing this with intention is by traveling alone to a country where very few people speak your language. This is a practice author James Clear has used to get himself accustomed to feeling uncomfortable and being OK with that. As Clear explained to me:

> By definition, you only know how mentally tough you are as what
> you have to face at the time . . . Until you are tested, you don't

know if you have that capability. So the purpose of voluntary hardship is to test that every now and then, so that you develop the ability to be mentally tough, and so that you know that you are capable of it. I view mental toughness [as being] like a muscle. It atrophies without use. If you just live a life of ease, then you fashion a mind that can only handle ease. Traveling is one way to do that."[2]

Discipline starts with yourself, by doing things like waking up early and making yourself stretch and sweat with exercise—and doing what others don't want to at the times they don't want to do them. There is no better arena for building the virtue of self-discipline and making it your own than what you do with your body: nutrition and exercise.

Now, I can almost hear the questions arise as I type these words: "What does my physical fitness have to do with my performance as a manager and leader at work?" The answer comes in two parts: external and internal.

Asking whether physical appearance should matter more than the substance of leading and performing is not an unreasonable question. Whether one thinks appearance should matter or not, *it does.* Whether people should judge others on their appearances or not, *they do.* And since leading is a results-oriented mission, I'm focused here on what *is* needed to successfully get others to follow your lead, not on what *should be* needed. Here, that means avoiding the contradiction of telling others to do hard things even as an undisciplined appearance indicates an unwillingness on the leader's part to do hard things. This matters because people don't follow undisciplined leaders for long. People stop listening if they sense you're a fraud. People respect those who practice what they preach.

More important than this external factor is the effect of physical self-discipline internally. In other words, the self-discipline with which you maintain your physical body will affect the minds of those you lead, but it will impact your own mind even more. This is about building yourself mentally to be tough in moments of adversity.

David Goggins is a retired US Navy SEAL, ultra-endurance athlete, and author of the book *Can't Hurt Me.*

I knew through working out, I started finding self-esteem. That's when doors started opening up. Working out is not a physical thing for me. It's a mental thing. I saw working out as a way for me to build calluses on my mind. I equate training to mental toughness. Waking up early, training, it looks horrible. It's uncomfortable. It's brutal. I don't want to do that. Through that, I found myself. I started seeing myself very differently from the average human being. It was a great never-ending work ethic. This is what created my self-esteem and confidence as a person."[3]

Mental callouses. Think about the value to a leader of the confidence built from doing things that are hard: waking up before everyone else, stretching your body, working out. The effect on your brain is about more than just mental fortitude. Your brain doesn't work at an optimal level when you have a fatty liver, if your blood sugar is high, when your gut is unhealthy, or when you have inflammation.[4] This is why it's important to eat a whole food, nutrient dense diet, and work out on a regular basis. It's not just about looking the part. It's about feeling the part. Dare I say, it's about *being the part.*

RESPONSE MANAGEMENT

A mind defined by self-disciplined thought is critical to responding to adversity. In his book *Shadow Divers*, bestselling author Robert Kurson writes about the riveting adventure of two scuba divers who risk everything to find Hitler's lost submarine. It's an amazing story, but what I found most compelling about Kurson's book was totally unrelated to history or hunting World War II–era submarines. Kurson explains the difference between the successful deep-wreck divers (an extremely dangerous profession) and those who died while diving. "Rarely does the problem itself kill the diver," Kurson writes. "Rather, the diver's response to the problem—his panic—likely determines whether he lives or dies."[5]

There isn't a person on earth who won't face adversity. Bad things happen. Adversity strikes. This is especially true for those who make the choice to lead. When you make that choice, you are now in charge of serving and helping other people. When issues arise and their lives get messy—so does yours. The difference between those who thrive versus those who don't is not about sidestepping adversity. Everyone will face adversity. Succeeding comes down to *how you choose to respond* in those moments of difficulty.

Failure is part of life. As Adam Savage told me, "I don't trust people who haven't failed."[6] If you're not failing, it means you aren't pushing yourself hard enough. When I left corporate America to run the newly formed Leadership Advisory practice at Brixey and Meyer, I was well aware that making mistakes, getting knocked down, and failing were inevitable. I knew it was part of the deal, as I was looking to expand my zone of competency. Several of the programs we've launched flat-out didn't work. I hosted a small workshop for a group of managers who were forced to go through it by their CEO. It was an epic failure. I had to take a step back and ask myself, "Why did I fail?" "What can I learn from this so that it never happens again?" I learned through reflection that I was not properly prepared, I didn't have my content fully fleshed out, and the group of managers had no desire to be there. They were compelled to go because their business owner told them they had to. The next time I hosted a workshop, I was prepared, with properly developed content and a great presentation. I also did more discovery on the front end to ensure the people in the room *wanted* to be there to learn and had an open mind. It's not about the failure; it's about how you *choose* to respond and learn from the inevitable adversity you will face as you strive to stretch and grow.

There is perhaps no more critical time than when the eyes of your team and others are on you, and failure reaches out and hits you in the face. "I do feel quite strongly if you don't experience failure at some point along the way, you're going to be more scared of it," says author

Sarah Robb O'Hagan.[7] "And as stakes get bigger, you need to have more of a tolerance for risk. I think failure is a really important experience to go through."

Bouncing back from failure is central to Sarah's story. After serving as an executive at companies such as Virgin, Nike, and Equinox, as global president for the Gatorade brand, and as CEO for indoor cycling studio company Flywheel Sports, Sarah launched her own motivational brand and book. But it wasn't any of those corporate successes that she pointed to when we spoke. Rather, it was the painful experience of getting fired. "It was one of the most horrifying, humiliating experiences. Packing up your box, everyone staring at me. I felt like a criminal." For O'Hagan, it was her response to that event that set the trajectory for her successful career arc. "The resilience I learned from it was remarkable. Years later, when I'm trying to turn around a $5 billion sports drink brand—a very public difficult battle—I tapped into that sense of resilience that I learned from the failures early in my career. Those experiences getting fired and making mistakes are so useful."

YOUR PRESENCE IS REQUIRED

I am fortunate to be able to say that my parents are among my biggest role models. Despite leading a business and working hard to build it, my dad never complained when my brothers and I asked him to play sports with us. As a kid, it never occurred to me that he might have just finished a 12-hour day—he never complained or begged off because of stress. If we wanted to go to the batting cages at 11 p.m. or shoot free throws at 5 a.m., my dad was there putting coins in the machine or rebounding our shots. There are many lessons worth drawing from those memories, but the biggest one for me is the simplest: to be a great parent, you *must show up*. It is your *presence* that matters to your kids far more than any presents you could ever give them.

The same is true for leaders of teams, and it is doubly so for new ones. Being physically present with your team is critical to developing a rapport with them, as well as a rich understanding of what they're facing. As a new manager, I remember finding myself chained to my desk on conference calls I felt obligated to attend. A wise mentor told me, "Get out of your office. Be with your team. You'll be pulled in many directions for your time as a manager. Remember, the most critical part of your role is coaching, teaching, and leading your team. You can't do that in your office alone on conference calls or reading email."

Great leaders know that being among the people they lead matters a great deal. Abraham Lincoln maintained a practice of hosting "ordinary people" in his office, where he would talk with them and listen to what was on their minds. He would take the time to listen to have these discussions *in person*. Frustrated by the effects on his schedule, Lincoln's aides tried to cut the presidential face time sessions short: "Mr. President, you don't have time to keep talking with these ordinary people."

"You're wrong." Lincoln would respond. "I must never forget the popular assemblage from which I have come."[8]

In a similar vein, Teddy Roosevelt spent three months out of the year as president doing "whistle-stop" tours (six weeks in the spring and six weeks in the fall). During these travels, Roosevelt would sit down with the newspaper editors who were critical of him to better understand their points of view.[9]

If the team you find yourself managing is remotely spread across the country, then make like T.R. and prepare to travel. *A lot. Get out* and be with them in the physical spaces in which they work, or don't take the job. Connect with them while riding in their car, experience the stress of rushing to the next appointment while sitting with them in traffic, and debrief the meeting over lunch at their favorite spot. You can't coach people by looking at a map. To avoid falling into this management trap, keep in mind this simple but profound idea introduced and popularized by mathematician Alfred Korzybski: "The map is not the territory." The description of the thing is not the thing itself.

Shane Parrish, a former defense security analyst and creator of the strategic thinking website Farnam Street, tells the story of General George S. Patton that illustrates Korzybski's maxim quite clearly. As

Parrish writes, "When he visited the troops near Coutances, he found them sitting on the side of the road, studying a map. Responding to Patton's inquiry as to why they had not crossed the Seine, the troops informed him that they were studying the map and could not find a safe place to wade across. Patton informed them that he had just waded across it and it was not more than two feet deep."[10]

You can't build a plan, a strategy, or a business without spending time in the territory. There's no better way to tell whether the river you have to cross is 20 feet deep or 2 feet deep than by wading into it yourself. Be in the territory. Show up. Your presence is needed to make better, more informed decisions. This will build credibility with the people you lead. Is it hard to travel to all the locations of your team members? Yes, of course it is. Managing a team is not for everyone.

But the challenge of presence isn't just for the managers of far-flung teams. For leaders of colocated teams, it's not as hard to be physically present, but know this: it's just as easy to come up with excuses for why you just can't do it. Fight the pull of those forces that would keep you away from face time with your people. Showing up for the people you serve and being there for your team builds credibility. Don't sit in your office all day on conference calls and writing email. Be *with* your team.

There are similarities between your work leading your team and leading as a mom or a dad. Your team at work (and your children) value your presence more than your presents. And if they don't, then you need to do a lot of reflective work on yourself to understand why. Your team wants clarity. They want their uncertainty to be moved to certainty. Your presence, and what you do while in their presence, will provide clarity and create more certainty.

MANAGING YOUR TIME

The great Peter Drucker plainly laid out the importance of how leaders work with the time they have, identifying it as the first of his five "habits of the mind that have to be acquired to be an effective executive."[11]

Drucker wrote, "Effective executives . . . do not start with their tasks. They start with their time. And they do not start out with planning. They start by finding out where their time actually goes." Knowing where your time goes and being strategic and intentional about what you spend your time doing represent a huge lever that turns efforts to lead yourself into successfully leading others. For Drucker, that meant applying a simple, three-step process:

1. **Recording time.** Much like tracking one's spending as a means of budgetary control, make an accounting of where you spend your time throughout the day.
2. **Managing time.** Remove the unproductive tasks that take time but don't produce value.
3. **Consolidating time.** Manage the *scheduling* of time so that "discretionary time" (when your presence or attention isn't required by someone else) occurs in the largest blocks of continuous time possible.

Without effort devoted to this process of time management, the natural currents of your organization will pull you away from valuable, productive work. Again, from Drucker:

> There are constant pressures toward unproductive and wasteful time-use. Any executive, whether he is a manager or not, has to spend a great deal of his time on things that do not contribute at all. Much is inevitably wasted. The higher up in the organization he is, the more demands on his time will the organization make.[12]

Consolidating your time into larger chunks is an underused approach whose value can't be overstated. It is only in these larger blocks of uninterrupted time that you can stay focused on a single task long enough to produce deeply valuable work. I'm a big believer in and a huge fan of Cal Newport and his concept of "deep work." In his book of the same name, Newport explains that "Deep work is the ability to focus without distraction on a cognitively demanding task. It's a skill

that allows you to quickly master complicated information and produce better results in less time."[13] Deep work is characterized by the
tasks that require calling upon your cognitive resources, harnessing
your creativity, and maintaining your focus. Conversely, shallow work
consists of the more mundane and mindless tasks that we can successfully accomplish without doing any of those things. Shallow work
includes tasks like answering email or attending meetings that are
related to our job but hardly productive in a tangible way.

When you perform an honest self-assessment, you may be surprised to find out how much of your time at work is spent doing
shallow work. And a life spent full of shallow work is a dangerous path
to mediocrity. That may sound harsh, but it is true. To make substan-
tial progress in work and in life, you need to focus on deep work in a
deliberate and meaningful way on a consistent basis. Literally, block
out time on your calendar daily to do this. As Newport so powerfully
put it to me when we spoke, "You should only do the amount of shallow
work needed to keep from getting fired, so that you have the time necessary to do the deep work that will get you promoted."

Get tactical on time management: Spend the last 30 minutes of
each working day planning the next day and the rest of the week.
Schedule at least one hour per day in deep work. While deep work is
typically not urgent work, it is incredibly important, whether for professional development (improvement work on yourself) or for a critical
work project. Put the phone away, and close your email application.
Devote full focus on the task at hand.

Being from Dayton, Ohio, I love learning all about Orville and Wilbur Wright's journey to create the first flying machine in their bicycle
shop on the west side of the city. Despite being severely underfunded
and undersupported in comparison with their contemporaries (both
in the United States and abroad), the Wright brothers aggressively pursued their goal in one of the most competitive professional landscapes
in the world (at the time).

Yet, even in the midst of this hectic race, Orville and Wilbur routinely spent long periods of time doing the kind of deep work that,

frankly, looked silly to onlookers at the time. Take it from John T. Daniels, a neighbor who ultimately took some of the iconic photos of the Wright brothers in flight. "We couldn't help but think they were just a pair of poor nuts," Daniels said. "They'd stand on the beach for hours at a time just looking at the gulls flying, soaring, dipping. We thought they were crazy. But we just had to admire the way they could move their arms this way and that and bend their elbows and wrist bones up and down just like the birds."[14]

When trying to build something that flies, why not watch something that already does? While standing on the sand dunes in North Carolina watching the birds appeared crazy to outsiders, it made sense to the Wright brothers. If the Wright brothers were able to dedicate time on a regular basis to stop building their machine in order to watch the birds, then I firmly believe all of us can and should as well. In fact, we can't afford not to. What is your version of watching the birds? How can you do a better job implementing deep work into your daily calendar?

HABITS: THE POWER OF SUBCONSCIOUS ACTION

Excellent habits help us be more consistent. Haphazardly going about your day does not lead to consistent performance. When I talk about habits, I'm really talking about consistency through the creation of a system or a framework of behavior. Your team will not be able to trust you if you are not reliable. Do they have questions about your ability to be present and ready to lead on a daily basis? If so, then that lowers trust and will hurt your performance as a leader of the team. Excellent habits lead to consistency, which leads to reliability, which leads to trust. It all starts with your daily habits.

Habits are important because they harness the power of subconscious activity. Army General and Manhattan Project engineer Charles C. Noble said, "First we make our habits, then our habits make us." Through habits, you enable yourself to perform tasks without jumping through the mental hoops and drawing from your limited reserves of willpower by having to *choose* whether or not to take the action before doing so. Waking up at 4:44 a.m. in order to complete my morning routine (stretch my body, drink 20 ounces of water, write in my journal, read, lift weights/run, have breakfast with my family, and drive my daughters to school) is not something I even think about anymore. It's part of my body's operating system now because I built the habit first. "We do not rise to the level of our goals, we fall to the level of our systems," says author and habit formation expert James Clear.

Creating a useful system of habits will benefit you in all aspects of your life. The habit of blocking one hour per day for deep work ensures that *learning* is part of each day. The habit of going through a gratitude exercise (writing 10 things you're grateful for) every morning will transform your mindset and spark optimism and energy for you as a leader of a team. As my dad always said, "It is your duty as the leader to be in a good mood every day." Nobody wants to follow a negative, cynical person. Through the building of useful habits, you will create a system that gets you in the proper (optimistic, energetic) frame of mind to lead people (and yourself).

> Habits are powerful, but delicate. They can emerge outside our consciousness or can be deliberately designed. They often occur without our permission but can be reshaped by fiddling with their parts. They shape our lives far more than we realize—they are so strong, in fact, that they cause our brains to cling to them at the exclusion of all else, including common sense.
>
> —CHARLES DUHIGG

WIN THE MORNING

Jesse Cole and his wife, Emily, bet everything on their dream: they created a new expansion team in the Coastal Plain League in October 2015. They started in an abandoned storage building, and sold only a handful of tickets in the first few months after coming to Savannah. On January 15, they overdrew on their account and were out of money. They maxed out their credit cards, sold their house, slept on an air mattress, and worked to make ends meet. Something needed to change. After reading bestselling author Hal Elrod's book *The Miracle Morning*, Jesse adopted the SAVERS method to "win the morning."

Silence. Meditation, prayer, breathing. Quiet your mind.

Affirmations. Encouraging words to tell yourself to achieve what you set out to do and overcome fears.

Visualization. Imagine yourself doing what you aspire to do, step by step. Then imagine the feeling of succeeding. (I practiced this a lot while playing sports. It helped me feel more at ease prior to a big game. I would even say things to myself like, "All I have to do is execute *my job*. I've done it thousands of times in practices and games prior to this moment.")

Exercise. Move your body. Sweat. Get the blood flowing. Dr. John Ratey, author of *Spark: The Revolutionary New Science of Exercise and the Brain*, says that "exercise improves your brain in the short term by boosting your ability to focus for two to three hours afterwards. This works on the cellular level through neuroplasticity, the ability of the brain to improve itself with blood flow and levels of brain-derived protein. It's Miracle-Gro for the brain, and it all comes from regular exercise."[15] According to researchers at Duke University, regular exercise can have as much of a positive effect on adults suffering from major depression as antidepressant medication.[16] Your brain remembers more when you move your body. In an experiment published in the American College of Sports Medicine's *Health & Fitness Journal*, students were asked to memorize a string of letters, and were allowed to run, lift weights, or sit quietly.[17] The students who ran were quicker and more accurate with their recall than those who kept to their seats.

Reading. Learn from others' experiences and lose yourself in a book. Put yourself in learning mode to start the day.

Scribing. Writing or journaling. This is a great way to document your belief system and create a more thoughtful mindset. It will help you be more self-aware and regularly spend moments in reflection.

Along with following the SAVERS method, Jesse also instituted gratitude as an additional aspect to his "win the morning" routine. He has written a thank-you note to a different person every morning for the past two years. In fact, I received one from him. It was one of the most thoughtful notes I've ever gotten, and I've been fortunate to receive a lot of very kind notes from fans of my podcast. Jesse's was very specific and exuded gratitude. In response, I was moved to immediately reach out to him, and we had a long conversation. It all began from his mindset to "Win the Morning" and start it with gratitude. The "Thank You" experiment started January 1, 2016. He started with gratitude right as the hardest times and biggest struggles were happening in Savannah. When I spoke with him about it, he said, "I learned during those challenges I had to be the best leader to myself, if I wanted to be the best leader for our team. I had to start the day on purpose and show up every day grateful for the opportunities I have and the people in my life."

In 2016, the Savannah Bananas were named the Coastal Plain League Organization of the Year after setting a new single season league attendance record. Jesse and Emily were named Coastal Plain League Executives of the Year. In 2019, the Bananas broke their own attendance record, extending their sellout streak to 100 consecutive games. In January, 2020, the Bananas announced that they had sold out all 2020 ticket packages.

PREPARATION: THE GREATEST
MEDICINE FOR FEAR

"By failing to prepare, you are preparing to fail." This sign hung in my football locker room at Centerville High School. Our coaching staff ingrained in our minds that our practices would be harder and more challenging than the actual games. This proved to be true.

Our preparation process began in the cold of winter—lifting in the weight room, running and conditioning work, and watching film as a team. Once summer arrived and school was out for our classmates, our workload only increased: 4:30 a.m. workouts (lifting, running), followed by fundamental skill work (throwing and catching), and reviewing everything on film. During the season, we would practice the same play over and over and over until we had mastered it. We practiced while we were exhausted. It got to the point that we could perform each play perfectly without even thinking.

When the time for our game finally arrived, we were so utterly prepared for it that we had nothing to be nervous about. There was no reason to fear whether we could execute our plays as designed; our muscle memory of doing so had been built through those thousands of hours of preparation. I was fortunate to quarterback the highest-scoring offense in the state of Ohio for two consecutive seasons. Whenever I think of a daunting task (like competing in a triathlon or giving a speech to thousands of people), I remember that "preparation is the greatest medicine for fear." Preparation is the ultimate confidence builder. Performing in the big moments as a result of that preparation turns that confidence into momentum, which is the first step to creating the flywheel to do it again and again and again.

When you lack confidence, your effective IQ and EQ go down because you're being self-conscious when you could be paying attention and thinking proactively vs reactively. It's one of the less understood aspects of a positive and productive culture— the conditions necessary to unleash someone's potential versus saddling them with the cognitive load of fitting in or impressing peers/defending what makes them different.[18]

What is your current process to prepare for a moment in which you will need to perform? As a manager, there are countless moments in which you will need to be excellent at your craft. Your willingness to prepare properly for these important moments is critical to sustaining excellence as a leader. Tom Peters pulls no punches and makes it as clear as few can: "Like it or not, boss, meetings are what you do. Every meeting that does not stir the imagination AND curiosity of attendees AND increase bonding AND engagement is a P.L.E.O/Permanently Lost Excellence Opportunity."[19] To stir the imagination and curiosity of your team, it takes proper preparation.

How will you open the meeting? What is on the agenda? What story can you share with your team to evoke the emotion and spark the ideas necessary to succeed that day? Most people are not excited about going to a meeting. How can you change that as a manager? How will you prepare for your one-on-one meetings with each team member? Have you thought about the unique qualities and personalities of each person and how best to connect with them? All of that takes prep work. It takes intentional effort and thought. To do it excellently, a manager must put in the time to *think* and be ready for the moment. One of my favorite quotes about this idea of being ready for the moment comes from Gettysburg hero Joshua Lawrence Chamberlain, whom we discussed in Chapter 2. He said, "We know not the future, and cannot plan for it much. But we can determine and know what manner of men we will be whenever and wherever the hour strikes."[20] You don't have to *get* ready if you *stay* ready.

Create a pregame ritual for yourself as a means of priming your mind to be ready to perform. For me, I have a couple of speech-only outfits. I know when I'm putting those clothes on, it's time to give a keynote talk. I do not wear those clothes for any other occasion. I listen to the same music, I do the exact same stretching routine in my hotel room, and I have the exact same note-taking process before my speeches (I write bits, thoughts, stories, bullet points, and transitions on a piece of paper taped to a manila folder). These may sound odd, but they prime my mind to know it's time to perform at the highest possible level. I owe that to my audience. As leaders, we owe that to the people we lead.

DETAILS MATTER

As a leader, there is no detail too small to care about getting right. On the way to leading the UCLA men's basketball team to a record 10 national championships over his last 12 years of coaching, John Wooden began every season's first team meeting the same way: he would teach his players how to correctly put on their socks.[21] He even demonstrated it for them. Coach Wooden would carefully roll each sock over his toes, up his foot, and around the heel before pulling it up snug. Then, he went back to his toes and smoothed out the material along the sock's length, making sure there were no wrinkles or creases. Coach Wooden had two purposes for doing this, he explained at an event honoring him. "The wrinkle will be sure you get blisters, and those blisters are going to make you lose playing time." Having good players lose playing time for blisters is how games are lost, and, Wooden joked, "your loss of playing time might get the coach fired." Second, he wanted his players to learn how crucial seemingly trivial details could be. "Details create success" was Coach Wooden's creed.

The Importance of a Quarter Step

In the beginning of 2006, I had been out of college for less than a year, having graduated the previous May. After a couple of NFL tryouts didn't pan out, I had expected that to be the end of my football playing days. A new career path lay before me in the corporate world of business-to-business sales. Then, seemingly out of the blue, I received a call from the head coach of the Birmingham Steeldogs of the Arena Football League. Suddenly, I had packed up my stuff and moved to Alabama to be the starting quarterback.

It didn't take me long to realize that the style of football in the AFL was quite different from what I had experienced to that point. To start, there are only three offensive and defensive linemen. This creates less congestion among the linemen, providing better opportunities for the defenders to get to (and hit) the quarterback much more quickly. Because of this difference, the Arena League had proven to be a great training ground for teaching quarterbacks to anticipate throws (throwing the ball well before a receiver is open) and get rid of the ball quickly (because if you don't, you won't get the chance to before you are sacked). Kurt Warner had famously used his AFL experience to reach the pinnacle of NFL success only a few years before, leading the St. Louis Rams to victory in Super Bowl XXXIV in 1999 and twice being named NFL MVP (1999, 2001).

To succeed in this new style of play, I needed to figure out how to create as much depth in my drop-back as possible but to do it in the same amount of time and using the same number of steps as I did when I played in college. To find the answer, I studied film of other AFL quarterbacks who had done it well. One tiny thing I started to notice was that some quarterbacks used what a basketball coach might call a "drop step." While under center waiting for the snap, these quarterbacks moved their left foot back about six inches from even with their right foot. This tiny little adjustment would create a staggered stance and give me a head start on my drop-back. In turn, this technique created more depth in my drop prior to me receiving the snap from my center. I would then pivot on the left foot and take my first step with my right foot, just like I had always done.

The result was dramatic. By changing this one small detail, my normal motion of dropping back to pass resulted in a gain of one whole extra yard of space between me and the oncoming rush despite taking the same number of steps (either a three-, five-, or seven-step drop). That extra yard of space created more time—about a third of a second—for me to find my receiver, anticipate his break, and throw the ball. That quarter turn of my left foot was the difference between me being tackled for a loss of yards and me completing a pass to my receiver for a gain of yards. Think about that: six inches led to a third of a second which led to a winning play instead of a losing one. Details matter.

How You Say the Words

An important phrase that my dad put into my mind from an early age was *"Never leave anything important to chance."* My job as a leader will be so much easier if I study the fine details of how we make a difference to the end user, and communicate this knowledge with power. Too many people never truly learn what their company does for the people they serve. It is extremely important to practice "how we say the words." Use the voice recorder app on your phone and say the opening words of your next meeting. Record it. Listen to it. How does it sound? Those *details* matter. Put yourself in your team's shoes so you can *feel* what is happening from the perspective of the people you are leading.

Too many take for granted the words they use, not understanding their power (for good or for bad if done poorly). Excellent leaders craft their vocal messages with great care, just like they might craft a proposal to a potential client. They do this to better understand how to get the best reactions. An example of this comes from the "magic question" in *Get-Real Selling*, by my dad, Keith Hawk, and Michael Boland. What they call the "magic question" was carefully crafted and finely honed by my dad after he grew weary of hearing "What keeps you up at night?" That lazy question has been trotted out over and over to clients by sales professionals for years. Instead, they propose asking, "What are those few things that absolutely must go right for you to be successful?" This newer, better version of the question was born out of my dad's practice of calling his voice mail and *saying the words* of his opening statement in a meeting.

I've found it incredibly useful to tend to the small details of human relations with the teams I've led. I utilize a "Get to Know You" document with team members and colleagues to better understand them as people. This has given me valuable intel, so that I can show love to the people who love my team member. I've built some lasting relationships with those I've worked with by sending their kids a video game from their Amazon wish list or some cookies along with a note that reads, "To Sarah and Jeremy, Your mom is absolutely crushing it at work. You should be very proud of her. I know she works hard to support you and your family. As a way of saying thank you, please enjoy these cookies and video game." Too many leaders neglect the tiny but important parts of serving the people on their team.

As a manager and leader, it is mission critical to constantly analyze and pay attention to the small details. They add up and can be the difference between success and failure. Some small details in your leadership role that matter: the manner in which you greet your team (smile, ask about each of them personally, be direct); how you start a meeting (Are you boring? Do you have a plan? Is it impactful?); the cleanliness of your desk; your process for organization. The list goes on and on. Small details matter.

No Detail Is Too Small

Jayson Gaignard is the founder of Mastermind Talks, an exclusive, invitation-only community for entrepreneurs. In 2016, I flew out to Ojai, California, to attend my first Mastermind Talks event. From the moment I arrived at the hotel, it was clear that deep thought had been put into the entire experience. A handwritten note from Jayson and his wife, Kandis, welcomed me to the beautiful property. For a first-timer like me, the event's first evening triggered a massive wave of imposter syndrome from knowing the caliber of people there, as well as hearing past attendees refer to "a family reunion" type of feeling.

Jayson makes his guests feel welcome with his careful attention to the smallest of details. When I got to my table for the first night's dinner, I found myself surrounded by attendees with whom I shared things in common. Each person at the table was a dad who had a background playing sports and spent time sharing their message from a stage as a keynote speaker. "I spend more time than I care to admit putting together those seating charts," Jayson told me later that night.

"But carefully choosing those 150 seats is *very* important to me. I work to create an incredible experience for each person. And that's hard. It takes a lot of time and effort."

Jayson's fanatical attention to detail doesn't stop at seating arrangements. After the midafternoon break at a recent event, I came back to my seat and found a box of Tagalongs waiting for me. The chocolate and peanut butter Girl Scout cookies are my guilty pleasure snack, which was one of the questions Jayson had included on every attendee's intake form. I looked up and around the room: each person had their own specific snack waiting for them at their seat. When organizing an event for 150 people, it's much easier and cheaper to have a set selection of granola bars, fruit, and coffee. *It's a lot harder when you care.*

Caring about the small, personalized details is what separates those who are pretty good from those who are excellent. Jayson lives by the "how you do anything is how you do everything" mantra, and spending time in his presence shows he lives that message daily by caring about the little details. I had a feeling he might after receiving my first email back from him (I asked him to be guest #1 on my podcast more than five years ago). In the signature of his email, Jayson displayed a quote from Danny Meyer: "Business, like life, is all about how you make people feel. It's that simple, and it's that hard."

Charles Comiskey, founding owner of the Chicago White Sox, once said, "It is the small things in life which count; it is the inconsequential leak that empties the reservoir."[22] Think about the tiny details of your team, the organization in which you lead them, the dynamics of relationships among peers, the meetings you attend and the ones you lead, the emails you write and the ones you don't respond to, how you *choose* to respond in challenging moments, the habits you are intentionally creating, the culture you are building, and the people you are hiring. Paying attention to them all is mission critical to your job as a leader.

KEY INSIGHTS

- Self-discipline matters greatly. Consistently showing that you do the hard things allows you to ask others to do similarly hard things with great credibility.
- Mental toughness is like a muscle that is built, or atrophies. Seek discomfort to stretch beyond your norms.
- People stop listening to you if they sense you are a fraud.
- It's not the problem that hurts you; it's how you choose to respond that makes the difference.
- Your presence matters, physically and emotionally. Your presence is required to make better, more informed decisions.
- Consolidate your time into large chunks, allowing you extended periods to do "deep work," enhancing your ability to focus without distraction on a cognitively demanding task.
- Develop great habits. Excellent habits lead to consistency, reliability, and trust from your team.
- Win the morning.
- Preparation is the greatest medicine for fear. Preparation turns confidence into momentum.
- How you say the words matters.

RECOMMENDED ACTIONS

- Create your morning routine. Write it down. Experiment with ideas and adjust accordingly for optimal performance.
- Keep a daily journal. Record your mindset during important events and how you chose to respond.
- Analyze your current preparation process for big moments (presentation, meeting with the CEO, a one-on-one with a team member). Ensure you've carefully and intentionally thought through the best way to perform at a high level in that moment.
- Choose and execute a new self-discipline for 30 consecutive days. For example, go for a 30-minute walk before dawn, read the *Wall Street Journal*, etc.
- Spend two weeks carefully recording how you spend your time at work. Identify and label "deep work" and "shallow work." Your aim is to free up and/or block out chunks of time for deep work.

PART II

BUILD YOUR TEAM

When I got the call telling me that I was being promoted to manager, I wanted to be ready to hit the ground running with as much positive momentum as possible. I sat down and wrote out my process, my plan, and my expectations. I began preparing to share all of it with my new team. But, before doing that, I knew it was supremely important *to listen* to them first.

I enlisted the help of my human resources partner. I urged her to *get as real* as possible with my team in uncovering their thoughts prior to me even starting. She met with my new team (without me in the room) *for hours*, working to get it all out. She asked questions like, "What are you most concerned about? What do you hope for most? What do you need?" She broke it down by individual, as well as taking a team-level perspective. This exercise worked in no small part due to her effort, as she was able to get the team to trust her with this information on the eve of getting a new boss. They shared what had worked for them in the past and what didn't. They discussed how I could best support them with the company's leadership. They laid out how to put them in the optimal position to achieve levels of excellence on a consistent basis.

Then I came into the room. Together with my human resources partner, they mapped out for me what a great leader/manager looks like *in their eyes*. We went over everything from the meeting together. The good. The bad. Everything. It created an immediate place of safety for the members of my new team to speak their mind. I took notes, and I took action based on what I was hearing.

Now, as the new manager, you can't recreate your principles and philosophy every time you are hired to lead a new team. It's nevertheless important to be a listener first and to find the places where your style and their recommendations can mesh. We all want to know that our boss listens to us and cares. We want to be heard. Doing this immediately helped build that culture of trust, empowerment, real, critical feedback, and openness. That formed the basis for how we would work together. We were pushing away from the dock, so to speak, embarking on a voyage *together*.

This is all part of the building phase: the work of earning the respect of current and future team members, and constructing the type of culture in which people want to do excellent work. From personal experience and the wisdom of others whom I've been fortunate enough to interview, I am convinced that cultures of excellence come from leading with vulnerability to create a place of psychological safety and empowering your team to have ownership over their work. The greatest teams I've ever been part of (in sports or business) had demanding coaches who created a sense of ownership in the team among the players.

It starts with understanding what it means to build an excellent culture, and *how* we, as leaders, work to do it and sustain it on a daily basis so that it lasts. That means creating a place where intellectual curiosity and creativity are encouraged, and understanding when tough decisions of change have to be made. The "how" part of that equation is hard, and we will discuss it. It's important to make it your own, with your (and your team's) unique personality so that ownership can truly be felt and be real.

As new leaders, we easily forget that the perception of us has changed. The company has given us a form of power in our new title. We must be aware of that and act accordingly. Understand how to use that power for good and serve your team. With any change, resistance will occur. How will we *choose* to respond in the face of that resistance? We must be ready. We'll talk about that.

We will also look long and hard at the most important decisions you will make as a manager: *who* you decide to bring on the team and *who* you decide to remove from the team. It will spell the difference in your career. The *who* is everything. We'll define what you should look for and, most important, *how* to find it—and how to retain your superstars. One of my ideas on how to do that may surprise you, but I promise you, taking this approach will be the best long-term decision you can make for you, your employees, and your team.

3

CULTIVATE THE
CULTURE

If you want a great party, invite great people.
—Marcus Buckingham
Bestselling author of *First, Break All the Rules*
(Episode #305, *The Learning Leader Show*)

THE ESSENCE OF CULTURE

Culture is an intangible, hard-to-define term, especially within a business. Do an informal poll of your colleagues, and you will probably get as many definitions as the number of people you asked. In my experience, culture is the combined essence of the people in the organization. Culture is not the Ping-Pong tables, or the color of the walls, or free snacks. It's the collective energy of the people on the team, in the organization, and within the business. The way we actually interact—the social system—results from the culture created by the people in it. And unsurprisingly, the leader is vital in setting the culture.

The origin of the word comes from the Latin *cultura*, which means "cultivate" and "care."[1] It's also derived from the Latin word *colere*, which means "to tend or protect." But culture means more than the etymology of the word. As anthropologist Clifford Geertz describes it in his book *The Interpretation of Cultures*, culture is easily confused with social systems. We need to understand them both to fully grasp what we mean when we talk about culture in an organization:

> Culture is the fabric of meaning in terms of which human beings interpret their experience and guide their action; social structure is the form that action takes, the actually existing network of social relations. Culture and social structure are then but different abstractions from the same phenomena. The one considers social action in respect to its meaning for those who carry it out, the other considers it in terms of its contribution to the functioning of some social system.[2]

Whether you've been paying attention to it or not, the culture of your team is being built day in and day out. Hopefully, the work of building your culture is intentional, but guess what? Whether it is the product of thoughtful design or mindless inertia, *your results will flow from the culture you build.* "The culture precedes positive results," writes Bill Walsh, legendary coach of the San Francisco 49ers and one of the greatest teachers in coaching history. "It doesn't get tacked on as an afterthought on your way to the victory stand. Champions behave like champions before they're champions: they have a winning standard of performance before they are winners."[3]

According to Daniel Coyle, author of *The Culture Code*, a great culture is something that can be taught, despite the fact that we tend to think of it as fixed.[4] We get culture from the people around us. Anthropologist Roy D'Andrade agrees:

> A good part of what any person knows is learned from other people. The teaching by others can be formal or informal, intended or unintended, and the learning can occur through observation or by being taught rules. However accomplished, the result is a body of learnings, called culture, transmitted from one generation to the next.[5]

It takes work to create an esprit de corps defined by a feeling of pride, fellowship, and common loyalty shared by its members. The responsibility for doing that work lies with the leader whose name is at the top of the "daily call sheet." In the movie business, the "daily call sheet" is the term used for the schedule of shots set out for the day's filming. That schedule informs the various actors when they need to be present on set for their scenes. When you're the lead in the movie, your scenes do the heavy lifting of the movie's story, so your shots are usually done first each day. Early in his career, actor John Krasinski received some advice from the legendary Robin Williams about the responsibilities of being "#1 on the call sheet." Krasinski shared the story with Scott Feinberg, host of *The Hollywood Reporter*'s podcast, *Awards Chatter.*

"One day he said to me, 'I think you're going to go far in this business, so the only thing I'll tell you is: one day, you're going to be #1 on the call sheet. Just know that's not a luxury. It's a responsibility, and that *your job* is to carry a set. So, you have to be the most energetic, you have to be the nicest, you have to be the kindest. Take responsibility. That is such an honor. And don't ever forget it.'" According to Krasinski, Williams didn't just preach about the lead's responsibility. He modeled it. "We were down in Jamaica shooting a scene and he said, 'You know, for instance, today the air-conditioning went out. But I'm not going to say I'm hot. Because if I'm hot, then the entire crew is hot and then we all sort of go downhill.'"[6]

A great example of how to build and sustain an excellent culture comes from Garry Ridge, CEO of WD-40. Through his time leading a one-product company, he's never laid off an employee, and his employee retention rate is three times the national average. A global employee opinion survey revealed that a remarkable 93.1 percent of employees at WD-40 are engaged, with 96 percent of them demonstrating trust in their supervisors. "The employees must feel they are in a trusted environment and among people who want them to succeed. We put the responsibility of the employee development on the leader," Garry told me.[7]

A big piece of WD-40's culture is the honest vulnerability of its leader. For Garry, the three most important words he learned through his time growing at WD-40 were, "I don't know." "As the leader, if you accept the fact that you will not know everything and surround yourself with a competent team and empower them to share their knowledge, it can create that magical culture we are looking for. I always listen with the intent of being influenced." He listens with an open mind, empowering his team to know that they can make a difference and have an impact on the business. In Garry's words, "I never lose. I either win or learn. At WD-40, we don't make mistakes. We have learning moments, and my big learning moment was, micromanagement was not scalable. And if we want to take this very beautiful blue and yellow can with a red top to the world, we had to build a culture based around a very clear 'why' do we exist, a set of values that set people free, and some strategic drivers that were easy to understand. And that's what we did. And now through the work of great people, we went from a market cap of $250 million, to now $1.6 billion."[8]

Garry proves that, in a competitive, tough market, being a people first leader was not only possible, but was the optimal way to operate. He was faced with challenging financials and refused to solve problems through layoffs. He innovated his way to prosperity and vowed to have 'at least *one more* employee' after going through the tough times. His mantra is "I'm not here to mark your paper, I'm here to help you get an A. I do not build failure into the mentoring of employees. Instead, I create a culture that encourages knowledge sharing and nonstop learning. The employees must feel they are in a trusted environment and among people who want them to succeed. We put the responsibility of the employee development on the leader." He did not assume that people were disposable assets to be shed in tough times.

EARNING THE RIGHT TO LEAD

In his video outlining the "secrets to great public speaking," TED curator Chris Anderson describes an idea as information encoded in a person's brain by a pattern of interconnected neurons.[9] The process of sharing ideas is a process of recreating that same pattern in the minds of your audience. To do that effectively, Anderson argues, you must do some work up front. "Before you can start building things inside the minds of your audience, *you have to get their permission to welcome you in*."[10] Speaking coach Lance Salyers tells his clients, "You have to earn the right to get inside your audience's heads. When they give you permission to do so, we call that 'paying attention.'"

The same is true for leading others.

Being "the boss" is not enough to command the attention and buy-in of the people you lead. Before you can start partnering with the members of your team to build the culture you want, you have to start by earning their respect. According to *Inc.* magazine, 86 percent of employees believe their productivity increases when they like their boss. The problem, however, is that three out of four employees identify dealing with their boss as the worst part of their jobs.[11]

One of the things I am most proud of about my experience playing quarterback at all levels was the effort I put into earning the respect of my teammates. As the first ever freshman to be named the starting quarterback for the varsity team at Centerville High School, I experienced at a young age the challenge of being the new leader of an experienced team. To do that, I was focused on showing up early, working incredibly hard, saying few words, being generous in sharing credit and always willing to accept the blame. Once I had built a year's worth of a track record, then I began to grow into my role as a more vocal leader. Heading into my sophomore year, coaches Bob Gregg and Ron Ullery told me it was time for me to "find my voice." "It's time," they told me, "you've proven yourself on the field. You've produced. Now you need to lead with your play *and* your voice."

I took that same approach to earning the respect of my teammates when I headed off to college. Two days after my last game as a Centerville Elk, I committed to attend Miami University in Oxford, Ohio. I called assistant coach Ron Johnson at Miami and said, "I want to move to Oxford the day after I graduate high school and work out with the returning players." At the time, this was not something that incoming freshmen did.

"Are you sure? Don't you want to enjoy your last summer before college?" Coach Johnson sounded incredulous at the thought.

"No, I have goals, and I will not reach those goals working out on my own away from my future teammates. I want to be with them." (By the way, now this is very common, as almost all incoming freshman athletes are expected to be on campus immediately after they finish high school). My pitch worked: the coach agreed and connected me with some teammates with whom I could stay.

The day after I graduated from high school, my dad and younger brother drove me to Oxford. With mist in all our eyes, we said our good-byes outside what was, even then, a dirty college house. I was now "in college," and would be sleeping on a spare mattress in the bedroom of two of my new teammates. I made this sacrifice because I had two primary goals during that summer that I thought would help me achieve my ultimate goal of becoming the starting quarterback at Miami. First, I wanted to earn respect with my work and not my words. I wanted to show my future teammates that I would be at every workout, working as hard as I possibly could right alongside them to get ready for the upcoming season. Second, I wanted to learn all of their names.

As a leader, you need to be able to look the people you lead in the eye and say the most beautiful word in the world to them: their name. And this is what I did. By the end of the summer, I had achieved those goals. I had built genuine friendships with my new teammates and had earned their respect as the only freshman who left his hometown two and a half months early to endure the hot days of summer work with them.

THE ELEMENTS OF RESPECT

Greg Meredith is the owner and president of Lee Plastic, a full-service plastic injection molding company in southwest Ohio. He is also a friend and colleague (LexisNexis & Brixey & Meyer). Greg and I have spent many brainstorming sessions discussing what it means to be an excellent leader, including the fundamental topic of how to earn respect. In mapping out a list of the keys to earning respect, Greg and I defined respect as regarding someone with high esteem because he or she has been deemed worthy. Over the course of time, we settled on the following seven keys:

- **Demonstrate competence.** You possess the necessary and critical skills required to lead in your organizational context.
- **Exhibit conviction.** You display assurance that the chosen course of action will lead to positive results.
- **Set high standards.** You aim high, both for yourself and your team.
- **Listen to your team.** You listen to feedback and you incorporate that feedback appropriately.
- **Work hard.** You put in the time and effort necessary to get the job done.
- **Do the difficult.** You do the hard things, like holding people accountable, confronting bad behavior, and staying true to your values even when it hurts.
- **Be consistent.** Your words, actions, decisions, and investments are in alignment.

RESPECT DEFINED

In 1940, then Lieutenant Colonel Eisenhower was a career Army officer with a good but unspectacular record. By the end of 1943, however, Eisenhower had ascended to the role of supreme allied commander in Europe, having been promoted through the ranks of colonel, brigadier general, major general, lieutenant general, and general in less than four years. He became a two-term president of the United States.

What drove this unprecedented rise? Eisenhower earned the respect of his commanders, his troops, and ultimately the citizens of the United States.

Demonstrate competence. Eisenhower excelled in the Louisiana maneuvers, a prewar exercise undertaken by more than 400,000 troops. This exercise revealed his talent for strategic planning and earned him an assignment in DC to work on US war plans. From there he had several critical assignments in support of the war efforts. This led to Eisenhower commanding the allied troops that invaded North Africa in Operation Torch, which earned him the right to command the invasions of Sicily and Italy, which in turn positioned him to be the supreme allied commander responsible for the D-Day invasion of Normandy. At each step along the way, Eisenhower proved his competence.

Exhibit conviction. Eisenhower consistently exhibited the confidence of his convictions and his chosen course of action. This confidence was on display when he frequently fought for contrarian positions. In 1920, he published an article "advocating that the Army make better use of tanks to prevent a repetition of the static and destructive trench warfare of World War I. But army authorities considered Eisenhower insubordinate rather than visionary and threatened him with a court-martial if he again challenged official views on infantry warfare."[12] In 1945, when President Truman was considering using the atomic bomb on Japan, Eisenhower took the dissenting view that it was unnecessary and threatened the goodwill that the United States had built up around the world.

Set high standards. Eisenhower's son David, also a career military man, eventually quit playing bridge with his father because he was such a demanding partner. Keeping up with Eisenhower was a challenge because of the high standards he set for himself and those around him. He had a high capacity for strategy and operations, and he worked to ensure that those around him met his standards.

Listen to the team. As supreme allied commander, Eisenhower had to deal with some of the strongest personalities in world history. British Prime Minister Winston Churchill, American Presidents Franklin D.

Roosevelt and Harry Truman, Soviet Premier Joseph Stalin, and a host of other military and civilian leaders were constantly seeking an audience with him. Eisenhower was able to listen to their concerns, balance their competing interests, and incorporate the most relevant feedback to deliver victory.

Work hard. Eisenhower's parents worked hard to feed and clothe their family of seven boys. In addition to the daily chores each brother was assigned, all of the Eisenhower boys found ways to earn extra money to help support the family. Young Dwight worked various jobs, from selling vegetables and his mother's hot tamales door-to-door, to laboring as a farmhand and working for several years at the Belle Springs Creamery. He managed these jobs while earning good grades in school and participating in sports and community activities, and this work ethic prepared him for military and presidential greatness.

Do the difficult. "Eisenhower had to take an unpopular step when he relieved his old friend George Patton as military governor of Bavaria because of the general's violation of orders against using former Nazis in government positions."[13] Eisenhower didn't shrink from making a tough call.

Be consistent. As president, the former army general was anything but a warmonger. In fact, Eisenhower worked tirelessly to create and ensure peace. He created an armistice that ended the Korean War and consistently deescalated rising Cold War tensions with the Soviet Union. His actions and decisions as president were consistently in the direction of building an enduring peace.

If you've done the work to earn the respect of your team, you will then be in a position to start building a culture you want to have. It's so important to have your team's partnership and buy-in on this effort. No matter how capable a leader you are in theory, you can't build a team or organizational culture by yourself.

While there are undoubtedly many different components to building a healthy, performing culture, there are three in particular that I value the most: trust, vulnerability, and ownership. When a work environment is set up with these three elements at its core, it creates a group of people who feel they can excel and take responsibility for the outcome of their endeavors.

TRUST

Trust is the foundation for everything you will do with your team. Yes, you will have to earn it, but it doesn't stop there. Equally important, and maybe even harder to do: you will have to learn to trust your team members. When you attain a leadership position, you are likely facing one of two challenges: you are either stepping into a position that some of your teammates wanted and competed for, or you are coming into a completely new team that doesn't know you well.

In the first scenario, how you've acted leading up to your promotion to a leadership position is very telling. If you've been a trustworthy coworker, it's a fair assumption that you will be able to gain the trust of your teammates quickly. Even assuming some of your team members are harboring feelings of resentment or envy, hopefully, you've earned their respect as a colleague.

Regardless of your entry point, as the new manager you will have to build trust and overcome the skepticism that's resulted from previous bad experiences. It's not unlike dating; when you start dating someone who has just come out of a bad relationship, you have an uphill battle to climb because that person will be less willing to trust someone new.

It's not just you. According to a 2016 survey, one in three employees don't trust their employer.[14] Stop and think about that for a second. No matter how good the play is that the coach calls in from the sideline, if three or four of the eleven players on the field don't trust the coach's judgment, that play is going to lose almost every time. The reasons for this widespread lack of trust in company management are both obvious and under the surface. According to management consultant Sue Bingham:

> Employees who don't trust their managers usually point to big-picture, obvious things: Their superiors skate the edges of ethical behavior, hide information, take credit for others' hard work, or flat-out deceive people. . . .
>
> Less-obvious causes of distrust tend to originate from the traditional environments in which leaders have been mentored than from specific behaviors of well-meaning managers. For example, traditional leadership training often focused on rule enforcement, which is akin to parent-child communication and not how trustworthy adults function. Today, leaders in high-performance workplaces don't write policies around the few bad apples; instead, they expect people to act in the best interests of the company and one another.[15]

Although Bingham doesn't mention Richard Branson by name in her *Harvard Business Review* article, what she describes is the leadership philosophy by which he runs his Virgin companies. "I think you should treat your people in the same way that you treat your family. You should have policies that follow through with that," Branson told Stephen Dubner on the *Freakonomics* podcast.[16] If team members want flexible work arrangements or the opportunity to work from home or abroad, give it to them, Branson argued. "People will give everything back if you give them the flexibility and treat them like adults." When Dubner asked how policies of flexibility lead to loyalty and productive results, Branson replied simply, "Because they feel trusted."[17] That said, depending on the work, sometimes it makes sense for the entire team to be in the office every day. Use your best judgment.

From the TED stage in 2011, retired four-star general Stanley McChrystal shared the story of failing during a command training operation at the Ft. Irwin National Training Center located in California's Mojave Desert. During the exercise, the company under

McChrystal's command got "wiped out—I mean wiped out immediately. The enemy didn't break a sweat doing it."[18] As he was preparing to get verbally ambushed by his battalion commander as part of the after-action review, McChrystal was surprised instead. His battalion commander said, "Stanley, I thought you did great." And in that one sentence, he lifted McChrystal back up and taught him that "leaders can let you fail, and yet not let you be a failure." For McChrystal, "a leader isn't good because they're right. They're good because they're willing to learn and to trust."[19] When I got to interview General McChrystal and ask him about the accelerating nature of trust among people and teams, here's how he answered:[20]

> Trust decreases transaction costs. . . . That's true in every organization. In the Pentagon, for example, it's full of really good people trying to get a good outcome. . . . A simple action can sometimes be just frighteningly painful. And the problem is, there's no evil person in this. They're just all trying to make sure they do due diligence. The problem is, you do due diligence long enough, and the opportunity passes, or the risk has already come and bitten you. So you've got to have this balance between how much risk you accept, and then how do you mitigate some of that. And some of that is in the trust. You develop trust bonds between people.

As a new manager, I worked hard to lead with trust, even though taking this approach meant opening myself up to getting burned from time to time. I have chosen not to be skeptical about whether people are lying to me. I live my life believing in the good in people because I think it's a healthier way to be. If I get burned, this creates problems, of course, and I deal with them when they arise. But I will rarely go into a relationship skeptical of someone's intentions.

Anabel Jensen, founding president of SixSeconds.org, said, "We can't be nonjudgmental. Our brains are wired to continuously make judgments. What we can do is notice the assumptions we're making, and reopen the case by staying curious."[21] Stephen M. R. Covey, author of *The Speed of Trust,* takes it a step further: "Given our brain's innate tendency to make assumptions, why not start with positive intent?" He goes on to say, "If we learn to assume positive intent as a start in any interaction, we'll see the world in a different light. I learned this from Indra Nooyi, the CEO of PepsiCo, one of the great leaders I've met. She said, the single greatest learning in her life was something she learned from her father, and that is this: to always assume positive intent."[22]

Is there risk involved in assuming positive intent or leading with trust? Absolutely, there is. But Covey writes, "If we don't trust people, how will we engage them, innovate, create, inspire, be a team? You can trust too much and get burned, but you can also not trust enough, and you wouldn't see the possibilities."[23]

VULNERABILITY

"Vulnerability sounds like truth and feels like courage," says researcher and author Brené Brown. "Truth and courage aren't always comfortable, but they're never weakness." Neither, then, is vulnerability.

Kat Cole, former president of Cinnabon and now the chief operating officer of Cinnabon's parent company, Focus Brands, is a wonderful example of this. After having the privilege of recording great conversations with over 300 top leaders and performers, my conversation with Kat remains among my favorites. During our talk, Kat explained how she quickly built trust by sharing vulnerabilities every time she went to a new country to open a restaurant:

> I think because I had to start traveling at such a young age and leading teams that I had never met, you learn the real trick to building trust. The real trick to building trust is giving trust, and one of the surest signs of giving trust is being vulnerable and telling people about yourself and being willing to be judged. And I had to do that because I had to get to know people quickly, which meant I had to let them get to know me. And so I learned, I

literally evolved over time, that when I go into a place and a team I've never met and I tell them my story, all of a sudden, I'm not just the boss coming in to lead the training, to lead the opening; I'm Kat, who grew up in a single-parent home, who dropped out of college, and who has worked really hard for what she has. And that's a totally different filter through which to view someone. And so I had to do it by necessity to build trust.[24]

Connecting with your team requires vulnerability because, as Jayson Gaignard says, "Relationships move at the speed of vulnerability." Vulnerability is about connection. People connect more with those who are open and willing to share where they're weak. I experienced this firsthand with one of my favorite bosses, Dustyn Kim. She was never scared to tell us the full truth even if it made her look weak or emotional. It made me want to follow her. It made me want to do a good job for her because of her willingness to be so open and honest by sharing her real feelings and thoughts. Among her many assets as a leader, Dustyn's willingness to be vulnerable was, in my mind, her leadership superpower.

I try to practice this in both my leadership life and my podcast interviewing work. If I want someone to tell me their life story, I must be willing to open up about mine. For example, early in the life of my podcast, I was interviewing Brady Quinn. Brady is best known as the former star quarterback at the University of Notre Dame, first round draft pick of the Cleveland Browns, and now football broadcaster.

Leading with vulnerability, I shared a story about my failures when I played quarterback. It was a 90-second story that unwittingly changed the dynamic of the conversation. Because I was willing to go to a place where we could talk about things that are uncomfortable, I made it OK for him to go there. And then he shared one of the most emotional and impactful quotes I had heard in years. He said, "Broadcasting a game from the TV booth (instead of being on the field playing) was like watching the love of my life marry another guy."[25]

As the leader, we must work to create a safe place for our team members to share truth. In order to gain trust, we must give trust, and the quickest way to build trust is to share your own vulnerabilities. The key to making it OK to be vulnerable is establishing an environment of "psychological safety." Dr. Amy Edmondson, a professor at Harvard Business School, defines psychological safety as "a climate in which people are comfortable being (and expressing) themselves."[26] Edmondson's research has illustrated the correlation between psychological safety and the better outcomes of quality improvements, behavioral learning, and increased productivity. An internal study conducted by Google found that teams with high rates of psychological safety were better than other teams at implementing diverse ideas and driving high performance.[27] They were also more likely to stay with the company. To give you added incentive, think of building a culture of vulnerability this way: by improving the way your teammates see their work environment, you would realize a significant reduction in turnover and in safety incidents, and an increase in productivity.

To build an environment of psychological safety, Jake Herwa, subject matter expert at Gallup, recommends asking yourself these four questions:

- "What can we count on each other for?
- "What is our team's purpose?
- "What is the reputation we aspire to have?
- "What do we need to do differently to achieve that reputation and fulfill our purpose?"[28]

OWNERSHIP

Creating a sense of empowerment in your team members is vital to the success of the team overall. It isn't just a fluffy buzzword that has little effect on the bottom line. A recent study found that disengaged workers had 37 percent higher absenteeism, 60 percent more errors, 18 percent lower productivity, 16 percent lower profitability, and 65 percent lower share price over time, among other negative results.[29]

It's very simple: people don't feel ownership if you tell them what to do. According to Gallup, only three in ten US workers strongly agree that at work, their opinions seem to count.[30] Retired United States Navy Captain David Marquet explains why this matters from his experience commanding the nuclear missile submarine *USS Santa Fe*. When Marquet took command of the *Santa Fe*, it was the worst-performing boat in the submarine fleet by multiple measures: performance ratings, crew reenlistment rates, and the number of officers who graduated to their own command positions. By the time Marquet handed the *Santa Fe* over to a new commander, it was the top-rated submarine in the US Navy.

According to Marquet, the key to this turnaround was in changing the way the *Santa Fe* operated from a "knowing and telling" organization to a "knowing and asking" organization.[31] If you're the kind of manager who tells your team what to do from the position that you know everything that's necessary and you know the right way to do it, you've created a "knowing and telling" culture. On the other hand, if you create a "knowing and asking" organization, you might know the answer and the direction you prefer your team takes, but you let your team discover that for themselves through dialog and encouraging questions. Instead of telling your team what to do, you give them the opportunity to figure it out on their own.

Think back to the last time you worked for an organization where you were told what to do and exactly how to do it every day. Did you feel any ownership in the work or in the outcome? Probably not. The most successful teams are made of people who have ownership over their decisions and their actions.

Empowering your team means that you're able to give them responsibilities and let them run with them, and then help them learn and grow from the experience after. And it isn't just the hard or unpleasant work that you need to learn to hand off to your team, but the plum assignments as well. In 2010, researchers found that leaders who were not only considered fair but also self-sacrificing inspired employees to be more loyal and committed themselves.[32] When employees feel loyalty, they are far more likely to be friendly and helpful toward other employees, which creates a self-reinforcing cycle. When leaders show they are willing to sacrifice themselves for the benefit of the team, employees are more productive and view their leader as effective and charismatic. While empowerment is the idea, effective delegation is the tactical way to realize the idea.

If you're used to being an individual contributor, the idea of delegation may feel counterintuitive. Empowering someone else to do the work is difficult if you feel they won't do it as well as you can. And often, they can't—at least not initially. However, your goal is to scale your team, your business, and your group beyond you. It won't ever scale beyond you if you never give your team the opportunity to rise to the challenge, to fail, and to learn. They may do it on a level that is not nearly as high as yours at first, but that gives you the opportunity to provide a critical feedback loop that will lead to improvement.

Additionally, it's important to empower high-potential people to lead training and coaching sessions. When I saw high-potential leaders, I made a habit of pulling them in to train newer team members. I gave them the opportunity to do the coaching and teaching, and then gave them feedback afterward.

Occasionally, I also selected teammates to lead group trainings and meetings. I might select the topic, but it was up to them to create the agenda and method of teaching. This created ownership among the team and primed them to become managers themselves, if that's what they wanted. Instead of relying on the leader to answer questions, are you empowering team members to make the decision and move on, within their project, within their assigned delegated task?

Ultimately, good delegation means eliminating bottlenecks and increasing the speed of growth of your team. In his bestselling book *One Mission*, former Navy SEAL Chris Fussell explains that on the battlefield, your team will be slow if they constantly have to radio back to their superiors asking for permission or direction.[33] Speed is crucial, whether it is on the battlefield or in the marketplace. Decentralized command and empowerment (empowering your team to make decisions without you) are imperative to your long-term success.

Tips for Delegation

• Start with an in-person conversation if you're in the same office. If not, set up a video conference.
• Schedule regular checkpoints and follow-ups throughout the project.
• Keep those meetings and make yourself available for guidance and feedback.
• Establish the best communication tool for questions that arise (email, team messaging apps like Slack, etc.)
• Set an end date/accomplishment point for the project.
• Hold an after-action review to give feedback.
• Document the after-action review.

Documentation of the framework is a critical aspect to ensure all team members know your thoughts and expectations for a task. This becomes vital if you find yourself having to put your team member on a performance improvement plan down the road. If they didn't complete the task or accomplish the goal, this will become part of their review. Whether it's positive, average, or negative feedback, it should never come as a surprise, so write it down. (Take it from someone who learned this the hard way. I initially didn't document those conversations, and it came back to bite me when human resources wanted my documentation to back up a firing decision.)

Managing your team is similar to parenting in that your goal is to teach your team so well that they eventually don't need you. A great example of this comes from Mike Krzyzewski, the head basketball coach at Duke University. I asked Steve Wojciechowski, one of his former players (and assistant coaches), why Coach K's assistant coaches routinely become great head coaches.[34] Krzyzewski is known for turning out great assistants who go on to lead their own successful teams. Wojciechowski said that Krzyzewski is the best delegator he'd ever seen. "He gives us specific parts of the game plan and we have 100 percent ownership over it—leading up to the game, in the game, and after the game," he said. Krzyzewski coaches his assistants afterward and helps them grow. The combination of trust and ownership leads these assistants to become head coaches in a short amount of time. That's the mark of a phenomenal leader: creating more leaders.

COMPETITION AS CULTURE

When I entered the business world as a sales representative, our culture was extremely competitive. The sales organization "stack rankings" were posted daily for all to see. The transparency of seeing each person's individual performance vs. their goals served to pit everyone against each other to drive revenue for the company. This is a fairly normal, even typically encouraged approach for a sales organization to take. It was all about competing with one another, posting the biggest numbers, being the best on the team. In fact, with that dynamic at work, you could hardly call it a team at all. We had little interest in working together or helping one another if it meant someone else got better numbers.

Competition can breed excellence, and I'm no stranger to intense competition. I may have performed well in that environment, but I could see the toll it took on people, and I knew it wasn't the kind of environment I wanted to be in long-term. Some went overboard in their enthusiasm to beat their teammates. I vividly remember one sales rep who was trying to close a big deal that would vault him to number one on the stack rankings. He was so excited when he got the deal that was equal to three months of his quota that he yelled and celebrated his success in his cubicle—but he was the only one celebrating. Nobody else was happy about him getting the deal.

I know it seems odd to think that nobody on his team was happy for his success, but that was the competitive nature of the culture and the environment. There was a zero-sum set up, meaning if he won, I (and everyone else) lost. Nobody else on the team benefited from his success. This created a "taking" culture in which there was very little knowledge sharing. When someone had success, they usually kept the insights into how they'd succeeded to themselves.

As much as it embarrasses me to admit, I played a role in perpetuating this environment because I saw no advantage to being a team player. Looking back, I believe some of this stemmed from my experience in college competing with Ben Roethlisberger to be the starting quarterback at Miami University. That was a zero-sum dynamic as well. If he won (which he ultimately did), I lost. He got to play, and as a result, I did not. No matter who you are and how good you think you are, there can only be one quarterback on the field taking the snap.

I learned as I matured and had the good fortune of excellent mentors (both in person and through books) that there was a better way. After realizing how frustrated I was by the big deal scored by my teammate, the lessons of those mentors snapped into place. I realized that there were other ways to get individuals to perform at their best. I decided that when I got to lead my own team in the future, I would create a different culture for that team to thrive in. With an eye toward that future vision of being a team leader, I started behaving differently right then as a teammate. I volunteered to mentor others, help teach them what I'd learned, and share best practices that contributed to my success. I wanted to foster a good working environment from within and create an ever-expanding ripple effect outward to the rest of the organization.

Choosing a Different Culture

When I eventually became the manager of the team, I set out to create a culture in which everyone could thrive and feel supported. The culture I wanted to build would be sustainable and enjoyable, and the team members would feel as if they were actually on a team, instead of just a group of individuals who were trying to beat each other.

I've played on winning teams, and I've played on losing teams. I've played for good coaches and for bad coaches. The best teams I've ever been on, whether it's in business or sports, are those in which the players cared deeply for one another, rooted for each other's success, and held each other accountable. In addition to talent and work ethic, the camaraderie of the teams I played on was the greatest determining factor of our success. I wanted to instill that kind of camaraderie into my work environment and my team. The best teams I've ever been part of had members that were empowered to lead by the coaches (or the bosses). These teams were player-led teams in which each person was held accountable for their performance by their peers, not just the boss or coach.

The change had to start with the people on the team: the *who*. When I stepped into my first manager role, our team had three open positions out of 15 sales territories. Running a sales team at 80 percent capacity can be devastating because of the lack of sales in the open territories, but I viewed it as an opportunity to bring in new people to start reshaping the culture, people who had high integrity and great attitudes to go with their ability to perform. My first two hires were grinders, very hardworking people who made up for any lack of talent in their willingness to persevere and improve on a daily basis. They were also teachers, and they took a lot of time to help the people around them. They were family-oriented individuals who demonstrated the same care to their teammates as they did to their families. They quickly became team leaders; they were involved in hiring, training, and building the culture.

The team formed a unique identity from within, and members exhibited pride in being on the team. The team chose a name—Team Hawk—and we hired a designer to create our very own logo, a hawk with a rusty sword. The rusty sword symbolized that our team was full of grit; we were grinders and willing to do what was necessary to succeed. It took on a life of its own after our leaders upheld and amplified our message. In meetings and at company outings, there were often speeches given by the leaders telling the origin story of our team, why it was unique and special, and what it took to be a part of it.

It was with this spirit of team pride and genuine support for each other that we created a "Stanley Cup" trophy using coffee cans and aluminum foil. This oversized trophy was passed along to the top performing rep each month. The winner got their name and picture added to The Cup, which sat on their desk. At the end of each month, we celebrated the cup winner as a team. There was genuine excitement for a first-time cup winner and healthy, happy competition. One of the most gratifying achievements as a leader was seeing the genuine emotions team members had for one another even as they competed with each other. This all started with the *who*, the people of the team, and their willingness to be givers and to truly uphold the values that we'd created. This is why the hiring process is vital to the long-term success of a team. All these small but important gestures drove the culture forward. (The team members are still good friends to this day.)

From then on, everyone that we brought on to the team contributed to its culture. Naturally, there were those who didn't like this change and didn't appreciate the new direction of the team. That was OK; they just weren't the right fit any longer, and they eventually left for new opportunities. For a while, the team's turnover *increased* because of the change in the cultural dynamic, but the end result was a group of people who all bought in and did their part to maintain a healthy, supportive, *performing* culture.

To foster the bond of trust and vulnerability within the members of our team, we needed to build actual relationships with each other beyond just being work colleagues. That meant I needed to be more intentional about our team gatherings and trainings. I found that when people got to know each other and learned about each other's families, personalities, and interests, they tended to communicate better with each other, feel more compassion for one other, and experience an increased desire to see everyone succeed. We traveled to Cincinnati Reds games together in a rented bus. We went to the horse track together, we saw movies together, and we did community service together. These activities built camaraderie among teammates. When you know someone on a personal level, outside of working together, you are better able to relate to them as your *teammate* instead of as your *competition.*

Ultimately, you want everyone to recognize that the team's culture is their culture, and that they each have a responsibility to maintain that culture through the choices they make, the behaviors they adopt, and by speaking up when others aren't doing the same. In my conversation with General Stanley McChrystal, he told the story of a young soldier in a unique battalion in the Army Rangers regiment who embodied this principle:[35]

> This unit was unlike any I'd been in before. It was very interesting. It was a very strict chain of command, in terms of rank and whatnot. But the standards of the organization were even more powerful than the rank structure. . . . I got there as a new captain, and I think I had been there just a couple of days. And a specialist—an E-4, a corporal equivalent, who is four to five ranks below me—came up to me and corrected me. I think I had my hands in my pockets or something like that. And he walked up to me and said, "Sir, we don't do that here."
>
> I never would've seen that in another kind of unit. One, because people would've just been too intimidated to do it. But, on the other hand, what we had there was a culture that said, "The standards apply to everyone, and everyone is responsible for making sure everyone else follows the standards." And so, this young specialist was absolutely right. I remember I was embarrassed when he did it, but I also said, "Guess what? I will never do that again because I'm gonna live to the standards that we all have here." I think that "truth to power" creates a place . . . not only where people feel comfortable doing it, but they feel like they have to do it.

We Want Givers

Adam Grant's book *Give and Take* introduced me to the research showing why givers (those who like to give more than they get) end up being more successful than takers (those who like to get more than they give) or matchers (those who maintain a balance of give and take, or quid pro quo) over the course of their careers. Grant's book also explored why a team full of givers would create the ideal environment for high performance and job satisfaction, thus making it a place where people would love to come to work. Givers are focused more on the success of the group rather than just the self. This mentality inspires trust in the motives of each person and creates an environment where there is an ample amount of best practice sharing without fear of exploitation (a taker stealing credit) or retaliation (when takers immediately criticize any idea that is not their own). How do we promote a giving culture? Highlight and reward giving behavior; set the standard by modeling the behavior with your actions. Be giving to other leaders in the organization outside of your team. Make it easy for people to give. It's all about environment design and reducing the friction for the behavior that will be most helpful. Initially set low bars for success and shine a bright light on the giving behavior. Make takers feel like it's time to make a change or time to leave.

Another major component I focused on was celebrating wins both big and small. Although I didn't think much about doing this when I first started out in my career, I had to learn to do it on a regular basis, both for myself and for my team. Celebrating wins became a big part of what we did as a team. I sent celebration emails to the team about an employee's big win, and then I would ask that individual to share how he or she did it. This not only gave that person credit and public applause, but it put them in a position to teach what they had learned from the process. If another teammate can take something from their success and use it in their own work, then it becomes a win for everyone. It was a telltale sign if a team member didn't like the emails; it usually meant they weren't up for the challenge of playing for a team. Gone were the days of employees celebrating alone in their cubicles.

We also celebrated when we met our team objectives. We set a team goal every month, and when we hit it, we would have a party. It's healthy to take time to celebrate. Teresa Amabile from Harvard Business School conducted studies on the effect of tracking small wins in performance. Teresa and her research team analyzed nearly 12,000 diary entries from 238 employees across seven companies. They found that tracking small achievements increased motivation by boosting self-confidence.[36]

If you and your team are just grinding forever, you'll quickly lose sight of the point—not to mention you'll see a higher likelihood of burnout in your employees. Toxic work environments affect more than just your confidence. Not only does this impact performance and job attendance, but poor health amounts to higher costs for both the employer and the employee. If you can develop a group of people who are genuinely happy for each other's success, trust goes up, the team becomes more cohesive, and job satisfaction improves.

PERCEPTION RULES

One of the interesting things that changes when you become a manager is the perception others have of you. This is particularly important if you have been promoted within your current company; more so if you've been selected to lead the team that you were once a member of. The instant that you become the manager, you are viewed differently than how you were as an individual contributor, whether you want to be or not. To build your new team's culture effectively, you cannot ignore this reality.

I am a person who craves feedback—the more specific, the better. When I say something that someone disagrees with, I want them to tell me so and I want to know why. I've understood these moments as opportunities to improve myself for as long as I can remember. When I became a new manager, I took for granted that my team would know this remained true about me and that they would continue to act accordingly. I was wrong.

Once, in a team meeting, I shared what I thought about an idea that had come up during the discussion. I gave my feedback and then asked my team, "What do you think? Is there a better way to do this, or should we go this route?" I asked with absolute sincerity. My team looked at me . . . and nodded. "Yeah, that is good," they said. I thought nothing of it, and we concluded the meeting.

Later in the day, a member of the team I was particularly close with came to me privately and said, "We have a problem. There are a few people on the team who were not happy with that meeting." "What are you talking about?" I responded. "I asked for their thoughts, and nobody said anything." I genuinely didn't see how these two facts— the team's silence in the meeting and their unhappiness with it—could both be true at the same time.

"Ryan, not everyone feels comfortable disagreeing with you. You are their *boss*." I was shocked. *Why would they not feel comfortable disagreeing with me?* I openly talked about my desire for a collaborative environment in which my team could share their true beliefs. And yet, it wasn't happening. As I thought more about what I was being told, I realized my oversight. I had done a poor job of understanding the situation from their vantage point. It turns out that the people on the team who did not feel comfortable speaking up had come from other jobs at which doing so always brought negative consequences. So they kept quiet, not wanting to risk history repeating itself.

Clearly, I needed to do better at considering each person's perception, understanding *why* they felt that way, and acting accordingly. It was a tough lesson to learn early on, but it forced me to get better. Don't assume you have the culture you want. Don't assume that everyone immediately feels comfortable disagreeing with their boss, even if you are explicitly inviting them to do so. People usually have reasons for behaving the way they do. It's *your job* as their leader to understand those reasons and respond in the most effective way possible to move forward as a team.

PUTTING THESE IDEAS INTO ACTION

Here are three practical suggestions for a new manager to begin building the kind of team culture you've read about in this chapter.

Get to know your team. It is imperative that you spend time with each person on your team. If your group is spread over a wide geography, this can be a daunting task. Know this before accepting the job. Your intention for these initial meetings is to listen, to learn, and to get to know each member of your team on a personal level. This happens in formal and informal settings. Meet in business/office settings where you discuss their work: what they do, how they do it, why they do it, their history, their ideas/thoughts on the future, etc. But make sure to also meet over a few meals at which there is no work talk. Get to know them as a person: their family life, their hobbies, what they are interested in.

Let your people get to know you. Be willing to share about yourself. The biggest fear associated with having a new manager is uncertainty. Help alleviate that fear by opening up and sharing more about yourself, your philosophy, your family, your history. Getting to know your team and having them get to know you takes time, effort, and careful thought. It is worth it. Your team will not care about your business philosophy or strategy if they don't care about you. And they won't care about it if they don't *know* that you care about them as human beings.

Always see people as people. Do not use phrases like "human capital," "head count," or "FTEs" (full-time employees) when talking about the people who work for you. Each one is a person who has a name. Never forget that as you progress up the management chain and you lead more and more people. It seems both simple and even silly to many in management positions, but the importance of this rule can't be overstated.

DEALING WITH RESISTANCE

Building a lasting, excellent culture depends on your ability to create an environment where people are willing to be vulnerable and to trust one another. When you empower your team and trust them to execute and learn from their mistakes, you create an environment in which it's OK to try something new, fail, learn, and move forward. As the manager, though, it's *also* your job to convince your boss and the broader organization to give you and your team the space to operate that way.

I know how easy it can be to decide that your hands are tied and there's nothing you can do. While it's difficult, great managers work to create their own culture *within* the business. It's critical that you think of your team as your business and take responsibility for what's going on inside of it, even as you must operate as an accountable piece of a larger organization. You can't control what happens outside of your team, but you are directly in control within your own sphere. Dr. Henry Cloud, author of several bestselling books and adviser to numerous CEOs, once told me, "You can't put your team in a bubble. You can't let a bad boss make you a bad manager. You can't use that as an excuse."[37]

If employees must check with dozens of people to make one small change, they will give up before they've even started. It seems easier to do nothing at all. Loosening your grip on your team can alleviate this, but what if it's *you* who are dealing with this from your superiors? As you set out to build your team's culture, you might experience the slow-moving effects of bureaucracy when it comes to making changes, or your boss might flat-out disagree with the culture you want to create. What do you do then?

It's important to be aware of perception. If you're dealing with an insecure boss who may feel threatened by you and your team's culture, be aware of this and adjust accordingly. As author Robert Greene told me, "You must never outshine the master."[38] Your job is to help your boss. Your job is to make his or her life easier. If you are known as someone who causes headaches or issues for your boss, you will only make yourself unhappy as a result of a rocky relationship. Or worse: you may find yourself unemployed.

During an interview with Liz Wiseman, bestselling author of *Rookie Smarts* and *Multipliers*, I asked her that very question.[39] She talks extensively about being a multiplier instead of a diminisher, so

I asked her what happens if your boss is a detractor and a diminisher. She said that she likes to think about how they got that way in the first place. It helps her become more empathetic because it makes her realize that they likely had some tough situation in their life that led them to behave the way that they do.

Beyond empathetic understanding, strategic thinking and communication will be required. A great manager understands that her role as the leader of the team is to sell her team's ideas internally about why her team operates in the manner in which it does. This can buy the team greater freedom and empowerment, with less micromanagement from above. That doesn't mean you sacrifice integrity by trying to hide what you're doing or flattering your boss to curry favor. The best way I've found to make this work is to focus on helping my boss see how my way of leading my team will ultimately help make her life easier and *make her performance look good to her boss.*

One of your jobs as the leader is to communicate exactly what you're doing and why you're doing it with your manager. Make certain your boss has vivid clarity on your leadership style, and why that mode of operation is leading to high performance. And show your gratitude. Tell your boss, "Thank you for your continued guidance, feedback, and willingness to create an environment for my team to be successful." Give your boss credit.

KEY INSIGHTS

- The *who* is everything.
- Surround yourself with a competent team and empower them to succeed.
- Create a place of psychological safety and empowerment for every performer to own their work.
- Micromanagement is not scalable. Making your team members all that they can be yields more than you being all that you can be.
- The top three components of culture are trust, vulnerability, and ownership.
- The quickest way to build trust is to share your vulnerabilities.
- Empower high potential people to lead training and coaching sessions.
- Good delegation with trust and empowerment eliminates bottlenecks and increases the speed of growth and the performance of your team.
- You can't let a bad boss make you a bad manager. You can't use that as an excuse.

RECOMMENDED ACTIONS

- Write down and analyze five people in your life for each of the following buckets: (1) ahead—people you look up to and go to for advice; (2) beside—peers who are on a similar path with whom you can speak honestly and in a nonjudgmental manner; and (3) behind—those you teach/coach/mentor.
- Choose three people on your team to lead an upcoming training session. Meet with them one-on-one to discuss the topic, desired outcomes, and how they will deliver the teaching. Help them prepare.
- Build a framework in which to conduct after-action reviews. Then conduct a review of a recent performance situation (a sale, a product development, a marketing campaign, etc.).
- Interview your boss. Schedule a meeting with your boss for the sole purpose of learning from him or her. Come prepared with great questions and ask follow-up questions.

4

MANAGE THE
ROSTER

*The most important question is Who? . . . Not what is your
next career step, but who are the people in your unit that you
are going to take care of as a leader? Take care of your people,
not your career. . . . I [found I] didn't have to have the answers
to the whats if I really paid attention to finding great whos.*

—JIM COLLINS
New York Times bestselling author of *Good to Great*
(Episode #216, *The Learning Leader Show*)

THE POWER OF WHO

The most important decisions you make as a manager (whether new or
experienced) are those about the makeup of your team. Surrounding
yourself with excellent people will be the single greatest determining
factor in your success or failure as a leader. Jim Collins, author of one
of the best business books of all time, *Good to Great*, put it succinctly
when we spoke: "*What* comes second. It's always *who* first."[1] My dad
told me early in my career that "hiring, training, and developing the
right people will make you rich and famous within your industry. Hiring the wrong people will make you dumb, poor, and unemployed."
Harsh though it sounds, I've learned that it's true. Building your team

well requires accurately analyzing what you have, correctly identifying what you need, and developing a deep understanding of what you're looking for beyond the simple skills needed to do the task.

A great example of keenly knowing what you're looking for when building a team comes from the days of NASA's greatest adventure: the Apollo Program's missions to the moon. Gene Kranz, flight director at Mission Control in Houston for the historic Apollo 11 landing and for the heroic Apollo 13 recovery, described the Apollo team as "a team that would not fail." Members of the group were carefully chosen according to their optimism. "Optimism is a collective construction, a view of the world based on a complex blend of what is and what ought to be."[2] The Apollo team studied people under duress. They studied their ability to communicate with others. They studied how they responded in times of acute adversity. If trainees didn't handle difficulty well, they were quickly weeded out. By the end of the training, Kranz said, "The team has come together, we've developed the ability to compensate for each other when the chips get down and we have an attitude so positive that given a few seconds we can solve any problem."[3] And on April 13, 1970, when the Apollo 13 spacecraft suffered a catastrophic, mission-aborting explosion in its cryogenic oxygen tanks, that "collective optimism" built into the team was what enabled Mission Control in Houston and the crew stranded aboard the crippled spacecraft to solve a series of almost unsolvable problems. Four days later, astronauts Jim Lovell, Fred Haise, and Jack Swigert splashed down safe and sound in the Pacific Ocean. Gene Kranz and the rest of the "collectively optimistic" team in Houston had guided them home to Earth against all odds. Those odds would not have been overcome if NASA had simply hired engineers based on their ability to do the math.

Even if you're not in the business of solving problems with people's lives at stake, it's still imperative to focus a great deal of energy on the *who* of your team. We've seen countless leaders who make poor hires. Rarely do they remain in those leadership roles for long. And those who do it well? They have the greatest odds of sustaining excellence over an extended period of time. Bringing onto the team a great new employee who is highly motivated and has the skills for the job can bring you great peace of mind and literally help you sleep better at night. Alternatively, adding a bad employee to the mix (or allowing one to remain on the team) can make your job more difficult, keep you up at night, and literally cost your company money. There is nothing we can do as leaders that is more important than taking the time and effort to hire well.

Warren Buffett is often asked for advice by business students. One of the questions he routinely fields is what he looks for in someone to work with. In response, Warren lists three qualities: "Intelligence, energy, and integrity. And if they don't have the last one, don't even bother with the first two. I tell them, 'Everyone here has the intelligence and energy—you wouldn't be here otherwise. But the integrity is up to you. You weren't born with it, you can't learn it in school. . . . You decide to be dishonest, stingy, uncharitable, egotistical, all the things people don't like in other people. . . . They are all choices. Some people think there's a limited little pot of admiration to go around, and anything the other guy takes out of the pot, there's less left for you. But it's just the opposite."[4]

General Stanley McChrystal echoes Buffett's sentiment:

> Sometimes you're successful just because you're lucky. And sometimes you're a failure just because you're unlucky. And, so, your relative wealth or promotions or any kinds of things aren't always directly related to either how hard you worked or how good you were. And yet, your character is something you can control. You can decide whether you're honest. You can decide whether you're loyal. You can decide how you think about duty. You can decide about all the things that really matter, and they can't be taken away from you. People like James Stockdale and John McCain taught us that, even in horrific situations like the Hanoi Hilton, if you can hold onto your character, you can hold onto that essence which is you, and nobody can take it from you.[5]

General McChrystal extended a gracious invitation for me to tour the hallowed grounds at the Battle of Gettysburg alongside the students he teaches in his leadership class at Yale. We learned a lot about the history of the battle over the course of two days with General McChrystal and some of his friends as tour guides. However, one teaching point that I specifically remembered was this, "The real lesson is . . . it's not tactics, not strategy; it's always about the people."

MANAGING THE TEAM YOU INHERIT

For nearly every management role you will ever earn, there will already be a team in place awaiting you. Unless you are in the position of building a brand-new expansion team, you will not have the luxury (and patience from above) of building a completely handpicked team. Chances are, the team you will be taking over will be a combination of high performers, low performers, and average performers. Knowing how to tell the difference requires more than simply looking at a spreadsheet.

You need a framework in place to assess the current team, their values, their performance, their motivation level, and the other critical qualities that will be key to the culture you want to build. It's also helpful to know why there was an opening in the first place. Did the previous manager get fired for performance? Did she get promoted for doing a fantastic job? Knowing why the job was available will help you more accurately assess the situation.

In his book *The First 90 Days*, author Michael Watkins writes about the challenges facing a manager taking over an existing team. When I interviewed Watkins, he discussed some of the biggest mistakes first-time managers make when they inherit a team. The biggest one is when new managers, eager to put their stamp on the team's makeup, do not properly balance stability and change. "Building a team you've inherited is like repairing an airplane in mid-flight. You will not reach your destination if you ignore the necessary repairs, but you do not want to try and change too much too fast and crash the plane. The key is to find the right balance between stability and change."[6]

As you assess the character and skills of your new team, you will (hopefully) find members who are obvious keepers. These are the people who exhibit all the characteristics you look for in a person and who perform at a high level. They exhibit intellectual curiosity, work ethic, coachability, energy, and integrity. They are group influencers and team leaders. As the new manager, it is critical that you make sure they "feel the love." By that I mean that you quickly signal to them that you see and understand the value they bring to the table and how important that value is to the team's success. Give them ownership in the team. Meet with them one-on-one. Ask them for ideas. Request their help. You may have been a high-performing individual contributor at one point in your career. Think about a time when you got a new boss. How did they handle the situation with you? Did they include you and make you feel valued as a leader of the team? If that wasn't your experience, remember how it felt and work to avoid creating that feeling in your new team's A-players.

Losing the team leaders' buy-in from the beginning could crater any chance you have of building a long-lasting, excellent team. Others on the team will follow their lead. Failing here will not likely cause the great performers to quit immediately. It is more likely they will begin looking for another job and putting in only enough time, energy, and focus to keep their current job, but nothing more. That is a recipe for the slow and steady death of a team, and it is an error that is perfectly avoidable.

HIRING: WHAT ARE YOU LOOKING FOR?

In order to build the right team, first, it is necessary to understand what you value in a person. The specificity of the role you must fill is obviously an important part of the equation. But, too often, hiring managers focus on those spec requirements as if they are the *most important* parts of the hiring decision. What's worse, sometimes those requirements are treated as if they are the *only* things that matter. Taking this approach is a huge mistake, and results in a great hire only by sheer luck. Far more important than the tangible skills you can find in multiple candidates or deliver through effective training is the makeup of the person who will be a complete asset to your team.

To get this right, you must be intentional. Here is a useful exercise I recommend to the leaders I advise: Sit down with your personal board of advisers—that group of trusted mentors we discussed in Chapter 1—and create your list of "must-have" or "nonnegotiable" qualities. Avoid the temptation to enumerate generically desirable virtues. For this to be an effective guide for your hiring process, you need to tease out *why* each of these qualities is important to you and your business. Here is my list of the values I look for when adding someone to my team, in no particular order:

- **Work ethic.** A willingness and track record of working hard to achieve excellence (common in athletes, military veterans, immigrants, and people who've had to financially support themselves from a young age, like working two jobs during college to pay their own way).
- **Resilience.** Ability to fight through tough moments in their lives during which they've been knocked down but they've gotten back up.
- **Humility.** Willing to ask for help. They don't think they have it all figured out. They constantly seek to be in rooms with people who are smarter than they are.
- **Curious.** Seeking not just information to expand their knowledge base, but wisdom to understand it. They want to know *why* and have mentors they regularly meet with.
- **Self-aware.** Knowledge of self and a willingness to take a hard look and honestly grade their skill level at particular tasks. They put measures in place to better understand themselves (mentors, assessments, dedicated time in their schedule to think, write, reflect, learn, grow).

- **Optimistic.** They believe, *If I consistently show up and work hard, good things will happen.* Their outlook is characterized by *pronoia*, which is the belief that the world is conspiring to work *for them* (or the opposite of paranoia, the belief that the world is conspiring to work against you).
- **Energy.** A zest for life. They lift up the energy of any room they enter. This does not mean that they are overly outgoing or even that they are extroverts. Rather, they have a magnetic quality about them.
- **Coachable.** This is why I've hired so many former athletes and military veterans. They are quite accustomed to being coached, especially in a critical manner from these experiences.
- **Effective speaker/writer.** Most jobs require a healthy dose of written and spoken forms of communication, so why not hire for it?
- **Dedication to a task.** Have they exhibited a track record of persisting long enough to make something good happen?
- **Thoughtful.** They take time to think, reflect, and analyze their actions and those of others.
- **Intentional.** They make choices on purpose. They don't live a haphazard life and say, "Oh well." They are still open to spontaneity, but they make it happen and have reasons for what they do. They are people of action.
- **Confident.** Self-belief that is the product of actual accomplishment in multiple life categories. They believe that they can apply their operating framework to any situation, implement it, tweak it, and they will be a productive achiever. This is not to be confused with empty bravado and arrogance.

You'll notice, the list isn't a short one. We human beings are complex, multifaceted creatures, and there are more factors to consider than a few generic qualities. On the other hand, this isn't a list against which I grade people to see how many boxes they check, with a predetermined number required to be considered. When I set out to hire a new team member, I am looking neither for bare adequacy nor for perfection. It is in between those two extremes that valuable compatibility lies, and that's my target.

Tech entrepreneur and investor Keith Rabois (a member of the "PayPal Mafia" along with Peter Thiel, Max Levchin, and Elon Musk) is widely known for his early stage investments and executive roles at PayPal, LinkedIn, and Square. He invested in Yelp and Xoom prior to each company's IPOs and is on their boards of directors. He shared his thoughts on how to make a good leadership hire, which I find instructive given his experience:

- Assess whether they think like an owner. Do they own mistakes? Are they kept up at night by what they would do differently if they were CEO?
- Are they capable of strategic thinking? Can they keep your entire business equation in their head and even come up with new levers you hadn't thought of that can move certain variables?
- Do their strengths align with the major risks of the company? Do they diversify your leadership team's style and background?
- Are they a magnet for talent? Can they bring on people even better than themselves?[7]

I share this with new leaders who are looking for direction on the optimal way to behave. What do the most effective leadership minds in business look for in a leader? Why do they look for these qualities? As Kobe Bryant once said, "There is power in understanding the journey of others to help create your own."[8]

Bridging the Gender Gap

In their book *It's the Manager*, Gallup's Jim Clifton (CEO) and Jim Harter (chief scientist of workplace management and well-being) highlight a Gallup study showing that gender-balanced business units—those that are closer to a 50/50 female-to-male split—perform substantially better financially than those that are lopsided in the gender makeup of the team. Combine gender balance with a high engagement culture, and the benefits are magnified. According to Clifton and Harter, there are a few reasons why gender balance improves business outcomes:

- Gender-balanced work groups have a greater capability to get work done and to meet customers' needs.
- On average, women are more engaged than men.
- Female managers tend to have more engaged employees than male managers.[9]

There's no other way to say it: if you want to succeed, be intentional about building a diverse, gender-balanced team.

Is Your Team Worthy?

How is your organization viewed in the marketplace? What is the culture? How well do people know about you and what you value? What is your specific team known for within the organization itself? What is your team's brand? The most effective leaders are thinking about this and are intentional about creating a team and an environment where people want to be. Everyone on your team is a member of your team's marketing department. Everyone is a recruiter, constantly on the lookout for great people to join your team. As Charlie Munger said, "How can you get a great wife? Deserve one." Are your actions those of someone who deserves a high-quality person to work on your team?

How Do You Find It?

After defining what you value in a teammate, now comes the hard part: figuring out how to accurately assess if the candidates you are interviewing possess those skills. Simply asking straightforward questions like "Do you have humility?" is not likely to yield any real insights. Those are the kinds of questions that typically generate the answers the candidate believes you want to hear. When it comes to the art of conversational interviewing, here are a few things to consider:

1. The interview is when candidates are on their very best behavior. If they're late for their interview, that is a big red flag that speaks volumes about their punctuality and what you should expect from them as a member of your team. If they can't show up to the interview on time, get ready for more of that behavior once they are comfortable and actually have the job.

2. Get them out of interview mode. Take the candidate to lunch or dinner. Walk around the office and speak casually. When you are working with a limited amount of time in an interview, it's on you as the interviewer to figure out how to be creative in order to get to know the real person behind the candidate. I've been on both sides of this. When I was considering a new job, I wanted to meet my (potential) new boss outside of the office to see what he or she was like as a person. I paid attention to how they spoke about other people (speaking poorly behind others' backs is a massive indicator for a bad boss), how curious they were, how much they truly listened to me, how often they looked at their phone, etc. In other words, how do they behave when they are more relaxed, and their guard isn't up because they're not sitting in "an interview"? You want to get to know the people you're surrounding yourself with on a real level, and not just as a "boss" or as an "employee" on your team.

3. Dig deep. Most candidates prepare for the basic interview questions. The best interviewers focus on the *follow-up* questions. If you ask a candidate to describe a time when he overcame adversity in his life (which we've identified is an important quality for this role), don't just listen to the prepared story and move on. Instead, keep going further. Ask, "Why? What happened next? And then what? And then what happened after that? And what did you learn from *that*?" I've

learned a lot about interviewing, both from the scores of job interviews I conducted as a hiring manager and from the over 300 guests I've interviewed for my podcast. In either case, without question, the really good stuff comes from the second or third follow-up questions. Rare is the occasion when the first question alone does the trick.

What Do You Ask?

It's critical that your questions in the interview align with the values you are trying to identify in a person. Each question should be asked with that specific purpose in mind. Based on what I value, here are some of the questions I have asked candidates I have interviewed:

Resilience. "Share a story about a time you failed/lost/struggled and how you responded in that moment." Once they tell you their story (and most candidates are very ready for this question), it is now on you to keep pushing. Ask "Why? What happened next? How did that impact you? What do you do now differently because of that?" Keep going, because what you are looking for isn't simply a *story* that answers your question; what you're really after is whether candidates truly have internalized the learnings from the experience they are describing into their personal operating system.

Curious. "What fascinates you right now? What are you studying? What's something you learned recently that really excited you? What books do you read? What are you interested in outside of work?" I want to see if they have a true intellectual curiosity. By that, I mean that they have a desire to aggressively seek to know more and to understand better. This quality is important because all roles are constantly changing, and if they are able to approach each change with curiosity, then their ability to learn, evolve, and grow increases.

Coachable. I ask them to share a story about feedback. Former athletes and members of the military tend to thrive in this area, but sports or the military aren't the only contexts in which people are coached. "Can you share a time when you've benefited from a coach/mentor/boss and how? How do you actively seek out feedback outside of your job and boss?" I want someone who craves feedback with the purpose of getting better. Do they *proactively* seek it out? That is my hope.

Effective speaker/writer. Often, I ask for writing samples. "Can you share proposals you've put together in the past? Do you have blog posts that you've published? Or a video of you giving a presentation?" At times I've given the candidate a pre-interview assignment in which writing and speaking are part of the homework. I want to see them *do the work.* Being an effective communicator is a critical skill for success in most roles today. We are on email constantly, we give status updates in meetings, we need to be able to tell our story and the story of our team. It's a huge plus to have people who can do this effectively.

Optimism/energy. This is something you can immediately begin measuring from the instant you speak on the phone, from when they walk in the door and how they greet the receptionist at the front desk. (I highly recommend regularly checking with the receptionist for information about job candidates. You can tell a lot about a person from how they treat people that they think they don't need to impress.) I want to work with people who believe things will go well and who bring energy into the building and into the team. Nobody wants to be around "energy vampires," as author Jon Gordon would call them.[10] We want people who bring a spark to the room. This is a quality you sense when you spend time with them. It's also worth asking their references and reviewing their social media channels for this behavior as well.

Do Your Homework

I'm amazed when I speak with hiring managers who don't check references at all or only one or two. When making a decision for *who* you're bringing on your team, it's *worth the time* to speak with as many people who know the candidate as you can. And not just the people they list as references. Use LinkedIn to see who they are connected to that they may have worked with in a past role. Reach out to those people to learn more.

Recently I sat down with Brian Koppelman to discuss how he puts together the team to create and shoot Showtime's hit TV show *Billions*. Prior to us recording, he gave me a tour of the office. As we looked in on the various "writers' rooms," I quickly noticed that it was a very collaborative environment. Not an open office space (we've read plenty about how ineffective those are), but an office with many rooms of people working together in small groups. When I asked Brian how he chooses the 150 people to work on the TV show, he said this, "First, we have a no asshole rule. If you're not kind, nice, and able to work with others, we don't care how talented you are, you will not be part of what we do. Then, since we need so many people, we really focus on the few key leader hires. We *have to* get those hires right. Because they are in charge of hiring the rest of the team. We trust those people to make great hiring decisions to fill out the rest of the group." As the cocreator and showrunner of the show, Brian doesn't have the time and/or mental capacity to hire everyone. I asked more about those key leadership hires. He said they have a number of meetings with them. Formal interviews, informal dinners, and, "Oh man, we do a ton of reference checks. Calling all the people they've worked with to be sure we're getting it right."

Search for your serious candidates on all relevant social media platforms. Look at their Twitter feed. What have they tweeted over the past couple of years? Are they speaking in a manner you would be proud to have on your team? Because when you hire that person, they now represent your team. The same is true for all social media posts. This may not have been a practice in the past, but it surely is now. The person is a representation of your team and your company. Their past performance and behavior is a great indicator of their future performance and behavior. The same goes for what they post on social media platforms.

FIRING: WHEN PRUNING IS REQUIRED

Having a garden full of gorgeous rose bushes requires more than just planting, feeding, watering, and enjoying the growth that follows. Healthy growth requires pruning from time to time. It takes a disciplined focus on the long-term health of the rose bush to take a pair of gardening shears to a growing plant. While it is painful in the moment, such actions are necessary for the bush to achieve optimal health and its full blooming potential. The same is true for the team you lead. Unfortunately, the act of firing someone and removing them from your team is sometimes a necessary part of the job. There will be times when the only path to sustaining excellence is telling someone that they will no longer be part of your team.

This is truly one of the most difficult tasks for any new manager. When it starts to become clear that a change needs to be made, you can find yourself feeling torn between conflicting emotions: wanting to be liked and be viewed as a friend by the employee while being respected by the rest of the team; wanting to *not* be like the harsh boss you may have worked for in the past while still maintaining the expectations and standards of the team culture you've worked so hard to build.

This is, without a doubt, one of my least favorite aspects of managing a team. But manage a team for any length of time, and you will have to do it, so it is necessary to understand how to do it well. Here are some tips on how to effectively make a change.

It Shouldn't Be a Surprise

Being terminated for unacceptable job performance should never come as a surprise. If your employee is performing so poorly that ending their time on your team is required, and they are truly shocked to hear this, *then you have failed that employee as a coach and leader.* The first time an employee hears in person from you that her work is not meeting the standards expected of her cannot be during the meeting in which she is being let go over it. Such a scenario is grossly unfair to the employee involved, and despite being obviously so, it happens with alarming regularity. There are also legal implications at stake. Wrongful termination suits can be brought against a company for any hint of impropriety. Document and be clear with the employee from the instant things start going south.

Most people do not enjoy giving critical feedback to another person. It is almost impossible to do so without worrying about harming the relationship. The solution for too many managers is not to do it at all. Even worse, however, is when the manager tells the employee that he is not meeting expectations, but uses language that is so softened to avoid causing discomfort that it comes across as too general to do any good. Hearing from your boss that "your work isn't good enough and needs to improve" is certainly an alert that something is wrong, but it doesn't give you any specific direction on what needs to improve and how. This is the worst possible outcome because the manager *thinks* he has given clear feedback to a struggling employee, so from that point on, failure to improve is deemed to be proof of the employee's lack of will or skill to get with the program.

The better way to deal with this is to be transparent with every person on your team—up-front from day one—that it is your *job* to be a coach. Coaches do not just give positive feedback. Great coaches give a full perspective of what they see and experience when working with each person as an individual, as well as the team as a whole. Along with this stated intention must come the promise that the feedback will be balanced, will be delivered from a good place ("I care for you and want you to be as great as you can be"), and that it will always be part of an ongoing conversation between you and the employee, rather than it just being their boss dumping bad information on them. If you've got the right people on your team, they will have greater respect for someone willing to give balanced feedback than the "cheerleader" manager who offers empty praise without regard to performance. People do not like uncertainty. They want to know where they stand. Tell them. Make sure everyone knows where they stand at all times.

By the time it is necessary to fire an employee, you should already have put in place some sort of a performance plan that outlines specifically what is wrong and—even more important—the specific steps and measurable progress the employee must show in order to improve. Ideally, this should be a written document that you, the employee, and someone from your HR department should sign, as dictated by your company policies. Your struggling employee should be getting individualized attention from you on a regular basis to measure the person's performance versus that plan. The goal isn't to be an oppressive burden on them, but to show them you are personally investing your time and energy into helping them improve. Firing someone is a huge responsibility, and should never be done with relish or zeal. It should be your last resort, only after all other avenues have been exhausted.

Involve Your Trusted Partners

Don't do this alone. Talk regularly with close mentors. Meet weekly with your human resources partner. Make sure that you are not missing any possible detail, either in the legal and policy requirements governing the termination of an employee, but also the good faith effort to help a struggling employee avoid this fate. This is a heavy burden to bear. As much as your company's policies will allow, don't try to bear it alone.

Write a Script

Stumbling on your words during a termination meeting can lead to bad consequences. It is not uncommon for employees to file wrongful termination lawsuits based on managers saying something they shouldn't have during the final meeting. Write your script, and share it with human resources, as well as your mentors. Once it's been deemed correct, stick to it. While I'm always an advocate of being human, real, and vulnerable, a termination meeting is one in which you should be mindful of your emotions.

Here are two things that you *shouldn't* say during this meeting, no matter how tempted you are to do so:

- "I completely understand how you feel." You shouldn't say this because it simply isn't true. You do not know how they feel, so don't claim that you do. Even if you've been fired before, this is not the meeting to try to find common ground.
- "I know this seems bad right now, but it will be for the best in the long run and you'll end up thanking me." No, this moment is not the time to tell someone to look for the silver lining. Getting fired typically generates feelings of embarrassment, sadness, fear, and anger. That is normal. Ignore the impulse to try to steer the person toward other feelings and a different perspective. News like this takes time to process. The best way to help is to allow them that time. Instead of trying to rush them through the emotional process, help them make as quick and as gracious an exit from the building as possible so that they can begin processing what it means for them on their own terms. It may in fact end up being what's best for them in the long run, but *right now* is not the long run. It's right now, and it hurts.

Here's How to Do It

Be direct, to the point, and share the news as quickly as possible. "The purpose of our time together today is for me to share with you that you will no longer be part of this team. And this is why . . ." When possible, share the exact reason why. If someone cheated, stole, or acted unethically, then tell them. If they were on a performance plan and were not achieving what was laid out in that plan, then this meeting should not be a surprise.

Involve the necessary players in the meeting. At a minimum, you should have a human resources partner present to act as a guide if you start to go off track as well as a witness to how the meeting was conducted. At times, you may even need to have a member of your company's security team present if you think the news could lead to a hostile response. I've had to do that before.

Once you have delivered the news and human resources has said their part, end the meeting and escort the person out of the building. There is no need to extend the meeting any longer than is necessary. If they have personal items at their desk, let them know you will box everything up and mail it to them. While this may sound harsh and even a bit melodramatic, taking this step protects you from an upset (now former) employee causing a scene due to high emotions and no longer feeling like there's anything to lose by expressing these publicly. That is not good for anyone involved. The employee who was just fired will most likely regret it, and the rest of the employees should be spared the distraction (at best) and the fear of being unsafe (at worst).

I learned this lesson the hard way. I once waited to fire someone who was not meeting the objectives of her performance plan. She was a single mom who was supporting herself and her kids solely on the money she made from this job. I kept putting off the decision because I knew I would be depriving her of that. I waited, and I shouldn't have. The termination meeting was awful, and she was confused. "Ryan, based on the performance plan, I should have been let go months ago. Since you didn't do it then, I assumed you never would." That was my fault. Through my extended inaction, I had inadvertently communicated to her that the expectations and rules had changed and that she had improved sufficiently to avoid losing her job. Hearing that this wasn't the case left her confused and hurt.

Additionally, my team lost respect for me and my leadership in that moment. My delay in making a change showed them that I would blanch in the face of a tough but necessary decision. They felt I let my emotions win the day, at the expense of the entire team. By avoiding this unpleasant duty of my job as a manager, I had sidestepped emotional discomfort while simultaneously putting the extra burden on them to make up for the underperforming person whom I was allowing to remain on the team. In the end, it's in the best interest of both the person and the team as a whole to hold people accountable to what you set forth in the plan that was designed for their improvement. Fail to do that, and the team notices that you are not a leader who holds people accountable, undermining the hoped-for culture of excellence moving forward.

Likewise, the underperforming individual also loses respect for you, even though you are letting him or her slide. You are showing yourself to not be a person of your word. Hard as it is to do, the best course of action is the consistent one. Make a plan, execute it, and hold people accountable. If they don't take advantage of the time and effort you are willing to put into helping them improve, then it's time for them to move on.

THE GREAT PERFORMER PARADOX

Building and leading a team of high-performing employees is a ticket to success for you as a leader. However, if you've managed a team of any size in any field for any length of time, you know how steep a climb that challenge is. With an understanding of what you're looking for and a disciplined, self-checking approach to how to go about doing it, you can get fairly proficient at finding *good* people. Even so, truly *great* performers are a rarity. Even one or two will take your team's performance to heights you will be unlikely to replicate without them, but finding them is hard. Be fortunate enough to do so, and this new level of success will bring with it a new management quandary: how to retain truly great employees, and—here's the paradox—*whether you should fight to do so.*

When a manager has hit the jackpot of finding great employees and has done the work of coaching them to truly great performance, losing such a person means having to start all over again. In the world of sales in which I managed, having a team member who, month in and month out, could be trusted to consistently overperform gave me the breathing room to devote more effort and give more time to other members who were still trying to figure things out. Take away that high performer's monthly work, and it wasn't just me as the manager who had to work harder. Everyone did.

But just as you wanted to progress in your career by growing into roles with more responsibilities and better financial rewards (whether within or outside of your company), the highest performing people on your team will want to do the same. The temptation for managers to discourage great employees from seeking greener pastures elsewhere is understandable. At times, this impulse serves to deliver wise counsel, as not every opportunity that appears better truly represents the next best step for your employee. When managers voice opposition to a high performer wanting to leave for a new opportunity, their resistance is couched in language reflective of the best interest of the employee or the team. But, all too often, the real issue is the leaders' concerns about *their own continued success.*

When I asked leadership guru Simon Sinek the question, "Why lead?"—why sign up for the extra burden and responsibility of leadership—his single-sentence answer struck me with the clarity of the purest musical note: "If you care to see others succeed, that's why you lead."[11] Few guests I've spoken with have ever said something I agreed with more wholeheartedly, and this issue gets to the heart of why. I believe in its proper form, the act of raising your hand to accept the responsibility (and benefits) of leadership is to volunteer to care more about the success of those you lead than you do your own success. Just like good parenting means preparing children to outgrow their role and leave the nest to go do bigger and better things, a leader knows that it is *our job* to lose our best-performing employees at some point.

Paradoxically, sometimes the best way to retain your top talent is to help them leave you. Instead of finding ways to convince or even prohibit top performers from leaving, try a different approach: *help them.* If you focus on helping others achieve what they want, you'll find that it will help you get what you want. When others in the organization see that you've created a place where people go to improve, get better, and ultimately get promoted, your odds of finding the next great performer will increase because those types of people will *want* to join your team.

As a leader, I really prided myself on helping the people I led do two things:

1. **Achieve award-winning levels of performance.** Being recognized in front of your peers is a gratifying experience for most. As a sales professional myself, I had experienced the thrill of winning our company's Circle of Excellence award a few times, and it was an extremely motivating event for me. I vividly remember being called on stage to celebrate a year of very hard work and hugging my colleagues in sheer joy. Along with the public honor came the gift of an all-expenses-paid trip to an exotic destination, which brought with it more opportunities for me to spend time with the leadership team of the company in a more relaxed setting. Being on that trip showed those executives that I was one of the highest performers in the company, which started building momentum for me to get leadership opportunities in the future. There are a lot of bonuses to individual performance success, and I relished the opportunity as a manager to help my team members earn those experiences and bonuses for themselves.

2. **Earn a promotion to the role that they wanted.** During my individualized, one-on-one meetings with each team member, we would regularly discuss their career goals and identify potential next steps for them to pursue. I talked about this with James Kerr, author of the book *Legacy*. James embedded himself with the winningest sports franchise of all time, the New Zealand All Blacks. His goal? To learn what excellence looks like from within and show how others could model their organizations after the All Blacks. "Rather than telling someone what to do, ask them what we should do together," James told me.[12] "People will rise to a challenge if it is *their* challenge."

During these one-on-one meetings with each individual on my team, my job was to be a great listener and understand the challenge that the person in front of me wanted to tackle. Once I confirmed that

I properly understood what they wanted to do and why, then we would work together to map out a path to get there. Along the journey to their goal, that employee would inevitably raise their performance and grow as a leader on the team, benefiting everyone in the process.

A great example of how that worked is Brent Scherz, who was one of my early ambitious sales reps and is now global vice president of inside sales for a multibillion-dollar international company. I had first mentored Brent when we were both individual contributors. Once I got promoted to management, I became his boss. Brent's desire was to earn a promotion to lead his own team. To get there, we started by laying out a plan to simply "get him in the room" for an interview. To do that, it was imperative that he perform at a high level in his *current* role. The next year, Brent finished as the number one sales rep, winning the use of a company-provided Porsche for a year as a bonus. This recognition put him in a position to be interviewed.

Next, he had to be prepared for the job he ultimately wanted. Beyond just helping Brent secure an interview, I began including him in coaching moments for the job of being a manager. For example, I would often do "mock calls" with members of my team, in which they would call me (acting as the customer) and go through their entire sales process, working toward a close (getting a deal signed). Afterward, I would bring them into my office, and we would break down what they said and did line by line on my whiteboard. During exercises like this, I would have Brent (or others I was helping to get promoted) sit in my office with me. Then he would lead the feedback session with the teammate. Sometimes this led to some uncomfortable moments, as hearing a peer deliver constructive feedback as if he were the manager can be awkward for all involved. But that's why I would do it. As a manager, I knew Brent would have to be able to do this, and there's no better way to prepare for it than to actually do it. Afterward, I would "coach the coach"—Brent then got to hear my feedback on how he performed as a coach to his teammates.

This experience helped him get the feel of what it was like to manage a team. As leaders, we must work to simulate the actual experiences of the roles our best employees aspire to as much as possible. This serves multiple purposes. First, it stretches a top employee and gives her responsibility above and beyond her current role. Great performers want to be stretched, pushed, and empowered. Second, it helps prepare them for when they interview for a leadership role, as it gives them real experiences to learn from and talk about. Finally, it helps them *be better managers* when they get the job. This is important because if you've done your job as their manager well, *then they will get the job.*

Recently I asked Brent what this meant to him at the time and how these actions made an impact on him. He said,

> Knowing that [my manager] thought of me as a leader and helped to develop my skills within the organization acted as a huge motivator for me. Not only did you provide me with an opportunity to grow for the future while within my current role, but you encouraged it and invested heavily in me doing so. This additional challenge of achieving above and beyond my "9 to 5" was a big motivator for me.
>
> Working with you, while I was still a sales rep, to help me facilitate the mock sales calls with the newer reps on the team was one action that allowed me to be more ready to take the leap into a management role, but also to improve my skills as a rep. Having the opportunity to listen and hear what good and bad sounded like from a different perspective was beneficial in my day-to-day as a rep. This allowed me to practice providing both constructive and critical feedback. I found this to be so beneficial, that it remains a core component of the sales culture where I work today, nine years later—focusing intensely on the notion that *practice should be harder than the game.*

Part of creating an environment where people want to do excellent work is having a track record of your team members growing into new roles and earning promotions. One of my proudest moments as a manager was when people like Brent earned a promotion. Their success or failure was something I felt responsible for (and still do).

It's much like a head coach helping his assistant coaches prepare to be head coaches themselves. The most excellent coaches have done more than just win championships. They have also created a legacy of other leaders—a "coaching tree" whose branches reach far and wide in their respective sports over time.

The name Bill Walsh is synonymous with winning in the NFL. After turning the San Francisco 49ers from perennial losers to the best team in the NFL, Walsh went on to win three Super Bowls. Even more impressive, though, is the success that other coaches have gone on to have after having learned the craft as an assistant coach under Walsh. Bob Glauber, a sportswriter for *Newsday* and author of *Guts and Genius: The Story of Three Unlikely Coaches Who Came to Dominate the NFL in the '80s*, wrote about Walsh's legacy, and how it all started. Here's how Glauber described it: "Bill Walsh was so upset he was passed over as Bengals head coach by Paul Brown (in 1976) that he promised himself that if he ever did get a head coaching job, he would make it a point to help develop other coaches. He started what I think is the most productive coaching trees in pro sports history, not just the NFL."[13]

After Walsh retired in 1989 after his third Super Bowl win, four of his disciples went on to win Super Bowl championships of their own as head coaches: George Seifert (49ers: 1990, 1995), Mike Shanahan (Broncos: 1998, 1999), Mike Holmgren (Packers: 1997), and Doug Pederson (Eagles: 2018). "[Walsh] knew how to train coaches and he concentrated on it and it meant a lot to him to see them become successful coaches," said Glauber. It is not an accident that Bill Walsh not only goes down in history as one of the greatest coaches ever, but his legacy lives on as someone who helped develop others into excellent leaders. As a new manager, it is never too early to start thinking about this and acting with the intention of developing future leaders. Your impact could become bigger than the mere performance of your team alone could ever achieve.

KEY INSIGHTS

- The most important decisions you make as a manager are about the makeup of who is on your team. *There is nothing you can do that is more important than taking the time and effort to hire well.*
- Take care of your people, not your career.
- Pronoia is the outlook or belief that the world is conspiring to work *for you.*
- Most job candidates are prepared for the basic questions. You will learn much more about them from your follow-up questions to their responses. Ask, "Why? Then what happened? What did you learn from that?"
- On day one as a manager be up-front that it is your job to coach. Inform the team that you will give a full perspective of performance feedback and that it will come from a good place, in that your desire is to help them achieve their best performance and all the positives that go with that.
- When terminating an employee, be direct, to the point, and share the news as quickly as possible.

RECOMMENDED ACTIONS

- Meet with your trusted colleagues and create your list of must-have qualities in the people you would hire. Take the time to flesh out why each of these qualities is important.
- Create your interview process and prepare your questions to give you the best chance to uncover the qualities you deem most important in the role for which you are interviewing.
- Schedule a meeting with a few of your mentors who have a lot of experience firing people. Ask them to lay out every detail and share the mistakes that they've made. Learn from their mistakes so that you're better prepared for when you have to do it.

PART III

LEAD YOUR TEAM

You've embraced the notion of leading yourself and have a plan in place to build a healthy team culture and a roster of people to bring it to life. All of the work you've done to this point is preparatory even as it is continual. Now, it is time to *lead your team*. How well you are able to do that will hinge on how well you master the art of being an excellent communicator. That means understanding the power of story and how to really connect with your team. It is through communication that the work of influence happens. Whether you are trying to understand how to effectively plan and run a team meeting or have a difficult conversation with a team member who is not performing at the level that's needed, skill in communicating lies at the heart of both.

It can be challenging for a top-performing individual contributor to make this change from taking care of your specific role, task, and performance to doing that for an entire team. Making the leap from player to coach can be drastic and dramatic. Now is the most critical time to get to know your team and understand what makes them go, because *making them go is now your job.* How well others perform is now the measuring stick for your performance. You are now responsible for steering the ship without getting to put your hands on the wheel. It's quite a different problem to solve.

And it all comes down to the results. As the leader, you are ultimately responsible for the results that your team produces. If you're not comfortable with that, then it might be time to rethink the choice you made to be a leader. We'll discuss what it means to have a vision, and why it's important. We'll discuss why you need to study and learn from your failures, but also why you should learn from your success so that you can replicate it (a critical step most neglect to take). We'll discuss the importance of leading, managing, and coaching, and the differences among them, and why doing all three with humility is the key to powerfully productive leadership.

5

SPREAD THE
MESSAGE

*We've built a culture of storytelling. We're constantly
surfacing, identifying, and telling stories at our organization.
There's always been an intentionality. Whenever I tell a
story, I'm always trying to connect that to a value.*

—Scott Harrison
Founder and CEO, Charity Water
(Episode #290, *The Learning Leader Show*)

Effective communication is the lifeblood of effective leadership. Michael Useem is a professor of management and the director of the Center for Leadership and Change Management at the Wharton School. Each year, he teaches an Executive MBA course in which he asks his students for an assessment of a person who best exemplifies ideals of leadership. Famous leaders in history are named, of course. But, often, the students offer up the names of leaders and bosses they have worked with. Of the many characteristics the students described that made those bosses worth mentioning, one stood out the most to Professor Useem: "Their exceptional capacity to articulate a plan and lay out a way of achieving it."

In other words: they were exceptional communicators.

What was true of the bosses of those business students was also true of the bosses of business leaders. Rob DeMartini was recently named CEO of USA Cycling. Prior to this new position, Rob served for almost 12 years as the CEO for New Balance, the athletic apparel and footwear company based in Boston, Massachusetts. While Rob was at the helm of New Balance, after a 20-year career as an executive at Procter & Gamble, the company grew its revenues from $1.5 billion in 2007 to $4.4 billion (as of 2017).[1] When I asked Rob about some of the exceptional leaders he has worked with or for over the years, two examples stood out. Of Procter & Gamble CEO A.G. Laffley, Rob said, "[It was] his ability to take a complicated message and boil it down into crisp words so that big organizations knew exactly what play had been called. He was very insightful." For Rob, clarity was also the calling card for Gillette CEO Jim Kilts: "He was a hard-nosed, tough minded, crystal clear leader. So you knew exactly what he wanted from you. That made it simpler to work for him."[2]

The importance of effective communication with your team cannot be overstated. As my dad has preached to me from a young age, "It is your job as the leader to be *vividly clear* when speaking to your team." They must understand the big picture mission of the team, as well as their specific role that contributes to the accomplishment of that mission. They must know exactly what you expect of them at all times. Your team can't know and do these if you don't clearly communicate with them. If the team doesn't have vivid clarity, then it is you, the leader, who is responsible for the failure in communication.

Some of the modes of communication that the effective leader must successfully develop and utilize to get his or her message across include:

- **Team meetings.** Planning and conducting a meeting so that the use of your team's time is useful for you *and* them.
- **Difficult conversations.** Understanding the importance of the occasional need to have a difficult conversation. Professionals appreciate directness and even critical feedback if delivered from the "My role is to help you be spectacular" point of view.

- **Directives from above.** Delivering a message to your team from organizational "higher-ups" that you may not completely agree with but are nevertheless responsible for carrying out.
- **Executive presence.** Having conversations at the executive level, whether reporting results up the organization and/or working to persuade senior leadership to take a preferred action.
- **Public speaking.** Building the framework for an effective speech, including how to deliver a one, three, and five minute "mini" speech.
- **Using the tools.** Making effective use of the communication tools at your disposal (email, phone, one-on-one conversations, etc.).

THE POWER OF STORY

Understanding and utilizing the power of narrative storytelling isn't about empty sentimentality and emotional manipulation. Nor is it a technique that is used *instead* of rational argument and solid facts. Rather, as researcher Brené Brown memorably said from the TEDx-Houston stage: "stories are just data with a soul."[3] Communication works best for both the brain and the heart when it covers both bases.

"Stories are how we think," says Dr. Pamela Rutledge, director of the Media Psychology Research Center. "They are how we make meaning of life. Call them schemas, scripts, cognitive maps, mental models, metaphors, or narratives. Stories are how we explain how things work, how we make decisions, how we justify our decisions, how we persuade others, how we understand our place in the world, create our identities, and define and teach social values."[4]

The power of a story's narrative structure isn't just in how it makes people feel or in how it moves them to action. Stories make information more memorable. In a 2014 study on listening, researchers played a series of videotaped instructions to the study's participants. For one group, the instructions were delivered in an expository form. For the other group, the content was conveyed using a story. The experiment's results showed a correlation between how the information was delivered and how well it was remembered: retention of the material was higher for those who received the instructions as part of a story.[5]

My favorite authors are the ones who deftly mix stories and science in a way that draws me in, engages me, entertains me, and helps make the point memorable. For example, in *Smartcuts*, author Shane Snow argues that lateral thinking—attacking a problem "sideways" by questioning "the assumptions upon which a problem is based"[6]—"is how the *most* successful people have always made it."[7] To do this, Snow uses stories as varied as they are well-told: from the effort of Snow's college roommate to shatter the world record for completing the video game Super Mario Brothers (6:28 vs 33:24 makes even the word "shatter" feel like an understatement) to a 16-year-old Benjamin Franklin using a female pseudonym to get his writing published in his own brother's newspaper. He shares these stories initially to engage and entertain the reader before he drops the science on lateral thinking and how and why lateral thinking can help put your career on warp speed. I followed up with Shane to ask more about his storytelling process and why it can be so impactful. He said, "My follow-up book to *Smartcuts* was *The Storytelling Edge*, which explored the neuroscience that explains why stories are so impactful. Turns out that when more of your brain is engaged, you remember the material better—and more of your brain lights up when intaking a story than when intaking facts. And even more awesome, stories trigger our emotions to cause a neurochemical called oxytocin to synthesize in our brains, which, crudely speaking, makes us have more empathy for whoever the story is about."

Now, of course, you're not reading this book to learn how to be a bestselling author or an award-winning Ivy League professor. So you may be wondering, "OK, those books sound interesting, and I will add them to my list of material to feed into my learning machine. But, how do I develop skills like that to use stories and narrative to better lead my team at work?"

Here are some characteristics of great storytelling that I've learned over the years:

1. **They are relatable.** The people reading or hearing the story must feel like they could be the protagonist of the story. They can identify with the situation and the characters.
2. **They have a hook.** As my friend Ryan Holiday told me (after reading my initial book proposal), "You must grab them by the throat . . . and make them want to continue turning the pages." Create intrigue right away and a reason for people to lean forward and/or keep reading.
3. **There is conflict.** There is a challenge to overcome. The protagonist gets knocked down and must figure out how to get back up. All this while the storyteller evokes compassion and empathy for the person.
4. **They tap an emotional nerve.** A great storyteller appeals to your emotions, understanding how word choice or tempo makes the audience *feel* the way that they do.
5. **They are simple.** The most intelligent communicators make complex ideas easy to understand. The least effective leaders take something simple and make it complex.
6. **They are surprising and unexpected.** The best novels and movies make you go, "Ohhhh, wow." When crafting your story, think of multiple avenues to get to the climax, and choose the one that will surprise your audience.
7. **They are satisfying.** Complete the journey for the audience. And share the reason why you told them that story and how it's applicable in their work and life.

To improve your own storytelling abilities, study someone who is skilled at it. Whether it's in books, movies, or podcasts, find the people whose stories move you and make you think. By studying other storytellers, you'll gain knowledge about storytelling as a craft. Try to emulate them.

HOW MUCH AND HOW OFTEN

How much you say can be as critical to having your message heard as how you say it. Brevity is important. It is the whetstone great communicators use to give their messages a honed, razor-sharp edge. The impact of what they are saying isn't dulled by the fluffy cushion of excess words.

To find out how an economy of words makes for a more effective message, talk to a stand-up comic. Comedian Bill Hicks advises would-be comics to "Listen to what you are saying and ask yourself, 'Why am I saying it and is it necessary?'"[8] These are two great questions that are useful beyond the world of comedy. No matter the audience or purpose, make yourself justify what you are saying and the words you are using.

Great comedians, writers, speakers, and movie directors know how to cut unnecessary fluff. When you are watching a movie that is the work of a gifted director, everything you see onscreen is there for a specific reason. A lot of time, money, and effort went into producing scenes and clips that never made it out of the editing room because they proved not to be necessary to telling the story.

How you communicate with your team or your boss should operate under the same principle. If you need to write an email to communicate an important message, take the same approach. Write the email. Then read it with the critical eye of a movie director. Ask yourself whether what you included is *necessary*. Force yourself to answer that question honestly about each key section and idea contained in the email. Then delete those parts that may be good, relevant, and interesting, but are not *necessary*. Do this every time you prepare to communicate, whether you're sending an email or prepping for a team meeting.

This is much easier said than done, I know. It is something I still have to be mindful of and intentional about, and I struggle to do this well from time to time. That's why it's helpful to get outside eyes on your work. For particularly important communications, have someone else read your message while applying their own measure of necessity.

Think of it like this: fluff wastes time, and as a result, people stop listening to you. However, when they know that you've carefully thought through everything you say, they'll stay tuned to your message.

Just as important as how much you say is the frequency and cadence of your communication. When you're a new manager, it is best to err on the side of overcommunicating with your team. Frequent communication can allay fears and build confidence as your team gets to know what you're about. They'll see that you want to hear from them and that you will do your best to keep the channel open in both directions.

Of course, there is a potential downside to frequent communication from a boss, whether new or not. You may appear to be a micromanager, or worse, *actually become one.* When I took over the reins of a national sales team as vice president of sales for a large multinational corporation, I was very sensitive to coming across as a micromanager to my new team. I wanted to show that I trusted my team and didn't need to be on top of them all the time, so I didn't want to distract them with emails too often or call too many town hall meetings. In my mind, they wanted to be left alone to do their work, so I erred on the side of less communication rather than more.

However, when I asked for feedback, I was surprised to learn that they wanted to hear from me more often. We had to work to find a happy medium. We set up a consistent weekly dialog about what was happening for everyone on the team. I set up regular one-on-one meetings with team members and blocked time on my calendar to travel and do "field rides" with individual contributors. In the end, my team and I settled on a regular schedule of consistent communication multiple times per week.

The mistake I made is an easy one to make. When taking a new position of responsibility for a team of people you don't know very well, the impulse to put your stamp on the team by micromanaging can be strong. In an effort to avoid this leadership sin, it is easy to overcorrect to a posture of silent distance. Neither of these approaches is good; it's your job to find a happy balance. How you structure your communication with your team depends on the company you work for, the level at which you find yourself, how many people you lead, whether you or your team members are remote, the health of the team and its ability to work together, and many other factors. If you work remotely, regular communication is even more important to make up for the lack of face time your team gets with you. In the end, a mindful focus and intentional effort are necessary to get it right, along with the transparency that comes from asking your new team for their input on the appropriate frequency and cadence of your communication.

Is it possible to have *too much* communication? In short, yes. You don't want your meetings and in-person discussions to be a drain on productivity. This applies to the amount of time and effort devoted to communication in all directions: between you and your team, but also between you and those in the organization around and even above you. The greatest piece of advice I received when I became a manager came from a mentor of mine. He told me that I would feel pulled in many different directions by other people from all parts of the business. "They're going to try to get you to go to all their meetings, both in person and on the phone, and your job is to spend the majority of your time with your team." He advised me to pay close attention to my time and say no to anything that didn't serve the direction of the team. Elon Musk has told his staff that if they can't add value to a meeting, and it isn't valuable to them, then they need to leave the meeting.[9] It may sound harsh, but it's a good rule.

CONNECTION

When it comes to communication, it's important to always remember its purpose: *connecting with other people*. Without the connective tissue of communication (whether through words, pictures, gestures, or even just a look on our face), we are all islands unto ourselves. We communicate to build relationships, express feelings, share ideas, and work together to accomplish what we could not do on our own. If you've ever felt alone in the middle of a crowd, you know the value and power of just having someone to talk to. Connection is why we communicate, and whether we connect is one way to measure whether effective communication has taken place at all.

Amy Trask is the former CEO of the Oakland Raiders and now a football analyst with CBS Sports. In addition to her television work, Trask serves as the chairman of the board for the BIG3, a professional three-on-three basketball league. Throughout her time as a female executive and authority figure in a male-dominated world, Trask understood how to quickly build rapport with those she worked with. Her advice to leaders in all positions centers on the need to connect with others. "No matter your industry, don't erect walls, don't build divides between various components of an organization," she told me. "The most important words when it comes to getting things done are: communicate, cooperate, coordinate, and collaborate."[10]

Connecting with your team goes back to having genuine curiosity and care for the people that you serve and lead. I love the way Herb Kelleher, the founder of Southwest Airlines, described it: "Communication is seeing somebody that works in your department and saying, 'Emily, I sure am glad to see you back. I heard you had a little difficulty with the baby. How's the baby doing?' "[11]

The key to connection is to avoid the (manager) monologue. Instead, the conversation is about helping the other person figure out the answer that will motivate them to move forward. While there was a chain of command and rules, I didn't run my team by telling them what to do directly. I wanted them to figure it out and feel motivated because they had learned the lesson for themselves. It took time for me to understand my own approach, but I would describe it as close to the Socratic method. I diligently asked questions of my team, but I'd start very casually. I might ask a team member, "What's going on? What's been good? What's not going well?" And I would keep drilling down and asking questions based on their responses, tone of voice, or body language.

I didn't see my role as the team manager as that of Chief Answer Provider. Rather, my job was to use communication as a means of stirring up my team's interest and creative problem-solving. By not filling the answer space, I gave them the opportunity to come up with the answers on their own.

Another approach to connecting with your team lies not in how *you* communicate, but in how you listen to them communicate. Researchers Jack Zenger and Joseph Folkman describe great listening as doing more than just receiving or even absorbing a message:

> While many of us have thought of being a good listener being like a sponge that accurately absorbs what the other person is saying, instead, what these findings show is that good listeners are like trampolines. They are someone you can bounce ideas off of—and rather than absorbing your ideas and energy, *they amplify, energize, and clarify your thinking.* They make you feel better [by] not merely passively absorbing, but by actively supporting. This lets you gain energy and height, just like someone jumping on a trampoline.[12] [emphasis added]

PERSUASION

Every day I spent in Birmingham, Alabama, preparing to start my post-collegiate football career, I followed the same routine religiously. If we did not have a game, I would wake up at 5:30 a.m., lift weights, and run. At 8:30, I would go to the arena to watch film, meet with coaches, and then practice. In the afternoon, I would sit outside in the hot Alabama sun and read (and reread) the one book I had brought with me from Ohio, *Influence: The Psychology of Persuasion* by Robert Cialdini.

I had purchased the paperback after being told that it would help me learn how to be a better sales professional. But in Birmingham, the book took on a new level of appeal for two reasons. First, as the quarterback of a team that I had just met, I knew I had my work cut out for me. I needed to build trust among my new teammates so that they would respond to me as their new leader. Being the resident "Yankee" (not something I'd ever been called before; where I'm from, it's just called being from Ohio) on a team in the Deep South, I knew I needed all the help I could get on influencing others and creating followers. Second, I knew that I wouldn't be playing football forever, no matter what happened with this unexpected opportunity in the Arena League. I recognized this as a chance to learn even more about leading in my natural environment on the field and in the locker room, so that I would be better prepared to lead people off the field in the business world.

Fast-forward to more than a decade later. Thanks to the opportunities resulting from my podcast, I was fortunate enough to finally connect with Dr. Cialdini and record an episode with him.[13] By then, his book had gone on to become a bestseller, with millions of copies sold. From his book and our conversations, I learned the principles for creating influence and persuading others. Because this skill is vital to success as a manager/leader, here are the three that I've found to be most effective:

1. **Reciprocity.** Look to give first before seeking to receive anything. Don't give and keep score. Don't give with the intention of receiving. Give to help others and serve them. Approach being generous in this manner, and the odds are high you will receive much more in the future from others in unexpected ways.

2. **Social proof.** People will follow you if they see others they respect following you. Involve the key people of your team early and often. Build genuine relationships with them. They are the influencers others will look to and ask for advice. Earn their respect by empowering them and helping them, and they will help you win the team as a whole.

3. **Consistency.** People are more likely to fulfill written, public, voluntary commitments. Just like goal setting, there is a higher propensity for the action to happen when it's in writing and discussed openly. Create a plan with your team and put it in writing. Then do the same with each individual person. Finally, make the commitments public.

HOW

How you communicate with your team will depend in large part on the way your workplace is set up and the cultural expectations of the organization. However, regardless of those specifics, I believe the best form of communication is done in person. Face-to-face interaction is the most effective at utilizing all of the tools at our disposal. Set aside for a second the question of having members of your team working remotely. Even when everyone is located in the same place, all too often, managers default to sending emails or making phone calls instead of getting up from their desk, walking down the hall to their team member's desk, and *talking* to them in a much more powerful and personal way.

This isn't a new observation, obviously. In their landmark management book *In Search of Excellence*, Tom Peters and Robert Waterman coined a simple phrase to describe this most basic form of leading others. They called it "Management By Wandering Around," now often referred to simply as "MBWA."[14] In the best-case scenario, a manager engages in MBWA multiple times a day. The purpose of MBWA is to connect with your people through the serendipity of random interactions, to gain a qualitative understanding of what's happening on the front lines. However, there is a fine distinction between successfully employing MBWA to better know your team and their work versus crossing over into the dreaded practice of micromanaging. Nobody wants to see you showing up at their desk when it feels like another round of The Boss Looking Over My Shoulder.

It was during my time roaming the aisles that I had my most effective conversations. These "micro-coaching" moments took place in the form of informal eight-minute talks, and always occurred as chance dictated. Rarely did they happen by premeditated design. So much of our team's bonding and (more important) learning took place during these moments. Scheduled one-on-one meetings with your team members are no replacement for this more casual communication format.

There is something powerful about learning by *doing*, and this is no less true when it comes to professional managers. Create moments for yourself to actually *do the job* that the people on your team must do. The best way to gain an understanding of how things work is to immerse yourself in it. The best way to learn is to *do* it.

Here is one example from my experience: As a telephonic sales organization, our team's job centered on cold-calling prospective customers. We would do a coordinated phone blitz, and I would join them on the phones. We would divide the list of prospects, and each time someone created an opportunity, we would share the news in teamwide emails. Doing better than the boss became a not-so-subtle motivation.

Additionally, I would sit in the cubicle of a team member and make calls on his or her phone to model the behavior. These sales calls weren't simulations or role-playing. There were actual customers or potential prospects in a live, totally unpredictable conversational environment. It energized the group when I got in the trenches with them, battled the nerves, and risked experiencing the same rejection they do. As the manager, this gave me invaluable insight into what my team was dealing with. I could hear exactly what the customers or prospective customers were saying on the other end of those phone lines: their objections, what they liked, disliked, etc.

Later in my career, I took over the leadership of a field-based team spread all over the country. This didn't mean I abandoned my MBWA strategy. It simply meant I had to adjust my tactics to the logistical realities. Instead of just getting out of my office and walking down the hall, I needed to get out of my city and fly across the country. Even though the frequency of these personal moments with my new team was much less than that with my previous teams, the intention and the effect were the same. What I used to do in the aisles between cubicles now occurred in the car or over meals. When before I joined the calling competitions, now I joined customer appointments in person, during which I asked questions aimed at uncovering what customers liked best and what we could do to improve. As before, I learned how to better lead my team by listening to them and the customers they served.

Most of the time you spend at work should be spent with the people you lead. It's like flipping the organization chart upside down: you're on the bottom and the people who report to you are on top. Even if you're not all in the same building, you can still structure your day in the same way.

If you're communicating with your team via email, remember that economy of words is essential. Have a purpose for every single email you send. If you start forwarding a bunch of meaningless emails with a note saying, "See below," the chances that your team will read them will drop dramatically. If they sense your emails have no point most of the time, your people are going to delete them and miss the important messages that you do send.

Feel free to make use of the wide array of communication channels beyond just email. As technology evolved and culture shifted, I started keeping an open dialogue with my team through text messages. The members of my current Learning Leader Circle are remote, and we use the application Slack to communicate in between the video meetings we have on Zoom. I've found this to be a useful tool for in-the-moment "burstiness," when a group of people are literally bursting with ideas, as Adam Grant would say.[15] We have threads on books, current events, issues, sales, and more, and it gives us a way to pose a question to the group and receive a wide variety of opinions quickly.

How to Deliver a Mini-Speech

Being able to stand up in front of a group and give a great talk will create more career opportunities for you than perhaps anything else you can do. This ability yields more credit from senior leaders than virtually any other professional business skill that you can demonstrate. And it's not just about being able to give a good speech. Perhaps even more important is demonstrating skill in handling tough questions effectively in group settings. It's imperative that you learn to be a great oral and written communicator. Joining the ranks of management will present you with many chances to either maximize those opportunities or squander them.

When most people think of delivering a speech, they think of the prepared presentation with a well-crafted slide deck that the speaker spent hours practicing. As a new manager, you may never be asked to give a talk under circumstances like that. However, it is likely you will be delivering a speech of some kind every time you meet with your team. You might have to give a one-minute, two-minute, or five-minute talk on a weekly basis. Knowing how to deliver a focused, concise, and impactful speech, no matter how long, is a vital skill.

Even if you're giving what seems like a simple one-minute opener to a meeting, you should put thought into it. Start mapping out your speech by clearly defining your purpose. Think about why the meeting is being held and let the answer guide what you say. From there, you are ready to outline the four basic components of a speech: a compelling opener (preferably a story), the main point you want to make, the information supporting your main point, and the summation and call to action.

A powerful story is typically part of a great speech. You will never have the attention of your audience as much as you do at the very beginning of your talk. If you can cultivate interest and pique your teams' curiosity early with a narrative that grabs their attention and engages their emotions, you can keep them listening through the rest of your talk.

Here is a framework to use as you draft a speech to deliver, no matter how short. The first comes from one of my personal mentors, Charlie McMahan. Charlie is the lead pastor at SouthBrook Church in Centerville, Ohio, and one of my favorite speakers. When I asked him how he builds his messages and weaves stories together in such a compelling manner, he shared with me his five-step process for teaching on stage:[16]

- **Teaser.** Share something that grabs the listener.
- **Tension.** Present the problem that your team or your listeners are facing. Let them know why this is important.
- **Truth.** What is real, usually supported by research/science.

- **Take-home.** The practical action step or takeaway that the listener can implement.
- **Together.** The inspirational ending that leaves them motivated to act. "Isn't this the kind of person we want to be?"

Regardless of what process you follow, the key to giving a successful speech of any length is being thoughtful about your preparation.

How to Have a Difficult Conversation

At many points in your career as a leader, you will be faced with difficult conversations. While there are many ways to approach this, there is one hard-and-fast rule: It should never be a surprise to someone that they are being put on a performance improvement plan, or probation, or whatever term your company uses. If your employee is surprised that you're having this conversation, then you haven't been doing your job as a manager prior to that moment.

It probably comes as no surprise that the primary feeling most managers experience when it comes to these conversations is fear. I was no different. I wanted everyone to like me, and I was nervous about sharing an unpopular decision. So I put it off. And I kept putting it off until the moment when I realized that I had a problem. I had two employees make a request for a territory change. In sales, this is common if a great performer is promoted; others are attracted to their old territory and will put in a request for it. Of the two, one was male and the other female. On paper, the male had more experience with the company and a longer track record of success. I gave him the territory. I told him. He was happy, and we got back to work. I never had the conversation to tell the other member of my team the bad news.

"Bad news doesn't get better with age." These words have been shared with me by more than one mentor in my career. On some level I was thinking that maybe it would get better if I didn't address it, but we all know that isn't the way it works.

Not immediately telling the other member of my team the news hurt her. She felt like I was playing favorites, and even made a comment about "the old boys club." I was crushed. I had made the decision based on past performance and rewarding the longer-term successful sales professional. But that's not how she saw it. This was my fault. Her perception was created by my fear of telling her the bad news. This was a mistake that took a long time to overcome. I had created a lack of trust with this team member, and fixing the damaged relationship took much longer than any discomfort I would have felt had I just been up-front and shared my decision and what motivated it with her *immediately*.

It became clear that the team had lost some respect for me because of my failure to communicate. I learned a painful lesson: there is a price for failing to act, and it doesn't only negatively impact the people directly affected by the decision. Failing to address questions in a timely manner also has an impact on the rest of the team, too, particularly a team of high performers.

Kim Malone Scott believes that if you care personally about your team, then you should be willing to share tough news early. As Kim said in our podcast conversation together, "It might feel like you are ending the employee's life, but that's a dramatic way to look at it. It's a temporary setback, and they are now free to pursue something they are happier doing in the long run."[17]

A piece of advice that I often hear is to approach difficult conversations with PCP: praise, criticize, praise. Although it might seem like a logical approach, it's not genuine if you don't truly mean it. *If someone needs criticism, don't sandwich it with fake praise.* You will lose credibility when it's time to offer them genuine praise if you get in the habit of using praise as a way to package negative feedback. Simply aim to treat each person with respect and deliver the news in a straightforward manner. They might not like what you have to say, but they won't dislike you for telling the truth about the situation.

This is especially true of great performers. They *want* feedback and will seek it out. They certainly expect it of their manager. High performers want to improve, and that doesn't happen without you providing that feedback loop for them. The greatest performers in the world hire coaches for a reason. They demand excellence of themselves, and they know they need direct feedback on a consistent basis. As the manager, this is now *your* job.

How to Communicate on Behalf of the People Above You

As a quarterback, I had to learn how to relay a message to my team with authority and conviction, even if I didn't believe in it 100 percent. At times, my offensive coordinator would call a play that I didn't like. However, I couldn't express that to teammates in the huddle as I called the play. I had to call it with confidence and a belief that it would work. If I called the play with indecision or my confidence appeared shaky, it was a virtual certainty that the play would fail. I had to spend that brief moment after I received the signal (the play call from my coach on the sidelines) to find a way to believe in the call, and then relay the message to my teammates in the huddle.

Doubting or disagreeing with your boss's decision will happen from time to time in the corporate world. There is no getting around that fact. As a manager, you will be given a directive to share with your team, a message with which you may not be 100 percent on board. While it's important to remain authentic and "never fake the funk," as Brian Koppelman would say,[18] a manager needs to confidently share the message. "Of course," you're probably saying right now, "but how?"

What I've done in the past is force myself to think through the directive, plan, or message from all points of view—mine and those above me in the organization. Only when I could truly see the issue from other points of view would I be ready to deliver the message to my team. This helped me remain authentic, but also not "throw the bosses under the bus." As a manager, you can't sell out the CEO and senior leaders. Not only are you prone to error (as you rarely, if ever, have all the information they do about the issue), but it is a surefire way to sow the seeds of a toxic culture.

One caveat that really should go without saying but is far too important to not say: if you are asked or told to do something that is illegal or immoral, then it's your duty to speak up and not blindly follow. People doing as they're told, even when it was obviously wrong, is how Enron and Theranos happen. Don't put your name on the long list of middle managers who sold their soul to not rock the boat, only to end up going down with the ship themselves.

How to Communicate with the People Above You

Communicating your message to senior-level executives in your company can be an intimidating experience. *What do I say? How do I say it? How do they talk in that conference room? Am I talking too much? Not enough?* The preparation process can be exhausting.

I once worked as part of a team that began preparing for a meeting with the CEO two months in advance. Countless meetings were spent agonizing over revisions to a bloated PowerPoint deck that was stuffed to the gills with information about every nook and cranny of our section of the business. The combination of people skills and hours spent on a simple message seemed both wasteful and yet necessary. The last thing anybody wanted to have happen was to appear unprepared to the CEO.

Finally, after weeks of frenetic preparation, the moment of the meeting arrived. The CEO skipped right over the crafted story we had wanted to walk him through and ignored most of the data we had included. Instead, he focused on only a few slides and drilled down on a few specific questions. Well over 80 percent of the work done in the previous weeks was utterly ignored. The material merited not a single word of acknowledgment in the meeting. I know this is not uncommon.

That unfortunate reality of corporate executive life notwithstanding, it is vital that you make the most of your opportunities when you find yourself in front of senior-level executives. You are representing your peers, your team, your boss, and others in your orbit. This may also be the lasting impression executives have of you as they are looking to promote people for bigger roles. Like anything else, there are exceptions to the rules, and every leader's personality is different, but here are a few tips that I've learned and gathered from others over the years:

- **Get to the point as soon as possible.** Unless they engage in small talk and show a desire for that, start the meeting by getting right to it. "The purpose of our time together is to cover . . ." Remember when we talked about economy of words earlier in this chapter? Almost every manager makes the same mistake when they're talking to an executive for the first time: they talk too much and take too long to get to the point. Not surprisingly, a combination of nerves and a desire to impress leave the manager unfocused. Strive to be concise and compelling, and be ready to answer any rapid-fire question the executive may ask. Above all, keep from talking too much.

- **Share the big picture and what it means.** Details are important, but don't go down a rabbit hole in the first five minutes when meeting with an executive. Learn how to present an "executive summary" and distill the essence of the message.

- **Prepare.** This should go without saying, but being overly prepared for the topic of discussion is a must. Anticipate questions the executive may have. Rehearse with a mentor and/ or someone who has held a similar role to those of the people at the meeting. "Preparation is the greatest medicine for fear." Know your material cold. Be a subject matter expert.

- **Be known as the go-to person on a topic.** The most effective way to build a real relationship with a senior-level leader is to be known as someone she can go to when she wants expert advice in a particular area. Most CEOs need to be generalists in order to run the company. Be known as *the* person who knows the most about that one subject that can fill a knowledge gap for that executive.

- **Be easy to work with.** Show up on time and prepared for meetings. Do more than what is asked of you, consistently overpromise and overdeliver (thanks to James Altucher for this advice). Always deliver on what you say you're going to do, work hard, and be nice to other people. It's amazing how far that alone will get you.

How *Not* to Run a Meeting

As a manager of others, meetings will represent a large slice of your communication time, efforts, and (hopefully) effectiveness. Far from being a necessary evil and mental afterthought, it is vital to get meetings right. Before we dive into that, though, let me tell you about the "worst meeting" I ever attended. I put "worst meeting" in quotes because what I'm about to describe wasn't a single meeting. It (sadly) happened more times than I would ever want to count.

I walk into the conference room as one of the invited attendees three minutes early. I'm the first person to arrive. As the clock strikes 9:00 a.m., less than half of the people whose attendance was listed as "required" are in the room. Finally, by 9:07 a.m., the rest of the group has finally shown up. Small talk fills the room until, at 9:12 a.m., the vice president who called the meeting finally arrives and takes his seat.

"Sorry, I'm late. I had an eight o'clock that went long. You know Jimmy doesn't know how to end a meeting on time. Anyway, how's everyone doing?" Quiet murmurs from the crowd. "Good. OK, who's presenting today? Can you hook your computer up to the TV screen, so we can see the deck you're presenting?" This question raises a slight problem: nobody sent out an agenda prior to this meeting, and nobody knows who is presenting or what is to be presented.

The vice president deftly shifts gears. "OK, Jessica, I saw that new product rollout deck that you shared in our other meeting. Can you do that for everyone in this meeting?" Jessica, left without any option but to comply, says "Um, I guess so." Seven minutes later, Jessica's deck (which has already been seen by more than half of the audience) is on the screen. She goes through it as the vice president looks at his phone and responds to texts and emails. Suddenly the VP pushes away from the table. "This is really important. I have to take this." He then leaves for a 21-minute phone call. Jessica powers through her presentation. Just as she is on her last slide, the vice president comes back in the room. "OK, was that helpful for everyone?" I am exaggerating a bit, but we've all been in meetings like this. As the manager, you have the power to change it. Be intentional about every meeting you host.

How to Run a Meeting

Let's now consider all that is at stake when you decide to have a meeting. Legendary investor and the creator of Y Combinator Paul Graham writes:

> The manager's schedule is for bosses. It's embodied in the traditional appointment book, with each day cut into one-hour intervals. . . . By default, you change what you're doing every hour.
> When you use time that way, it's merely a practical problem to meet with someone. Find an open slot in your schedule, book them, and you're done. Most powerful people are on the manager's schedule. It's the schedule of command.[19]

The other group of people, the ones who report to you, actually make things. They are on the "maker's schedule." "When you're operating on the maker's schedule, meetings are a disaster. A single meeting can blow a whole afternoon," says Graham. A meeting dropped into the middle of the afternoon breaks the remaining parts of the afternoon into segments that are too short to get anything of consequence done. "It doesn't merely cause you to switch from one task to another; it changes the mode in which you work."

I am not proposing that we outlaw meetings or get rid of them completely. As a leader, you need to meet with your team. I'm arguing that we must be more mindful of a few fundamental questions way before the actual meeting:

- *Why* are we having this specific meeting? Is it *really* necessary? Are we having it merely out of mindless habit and unchecked inertia?
- *What* is the goal of this meeting? What absolutely must go right in this meeting to make it successful?
- *Who* needs to be in the room? Only invite the people who need to be there.
- *When* will this meeting take place? As Graham points out, this is perhaps more important than most people realize. In order to create as much uninterrupted time for getting work done as possible, can the meeting take place at 8 a.m. or 4 p.m.?

Regardless of the industry you work in, you want your team to be full of makers. Whether they are selling a product or working on a project, creating an environment with the most uninterrupted time possible (a maker's schedule) will put them in the best possible position to succeed. As the leader, *you* are responsible for the result. It is your job to do everything within your power to foster an environment of excellence for your team.

Unfortunately, most meetings don't proceed by design born of thoughtful consideration. Too many managers simply book time on their entire team's calendar for every Monday morning at 10 because that's what their boss did. And even though the team meeting is on the calendar at the same time every week into the far-flung future, they still end up scrambling to put together an agenda 15 minutes prior to the start of the meeting. Then, once the meeting begins (usually not on time), the manager slowly wanders through the opening ("hey, how was your weekend?"), and meanders through the middle and end until everyone's free to leave at 11. The result? The entire first half of the first day of the week has been wasted because "that's just how we've done it here." Break the cycle. Do it better. Be known as someone who has incredible meetings. And if you don't have a reason to meet, by all means, cancel the meeting.

Here are my rules for running a productive meeting, honed from years of suffering when it was done poorly and thriving when it was done well:

Be on time. Every time. No exceptions. The leader sets the tone for the meeting. *Never* be late. Block the 30 minutes (on your calendar) prior to the meeting to ensure this happens. (More on this in a bit.)

"Honor the present." Start the meeting on time, no matter what. Don't say, "We'll wait a few minutes for John and Suzy to get here." Start every meeting on time, and your attendees will quickly learn that they cannot be late to your meetings.

"No agenda, no attenda." When it comes to running meetings, I love how bestselling author Cameron Herold puts it in his book *Meetings Suck*: "No agenda, no attenda." Prior to the meeting, send a detailed outline of the topics that will be discussed. It doesn't have to be long, although Amazon founder Jeff Bezos is famous for sending a six-page Word document to every attendee before a meeting with the full expectation that they read it. The point is that what you send out is not only going to help your team prepare for the meeting, it will help you keep the meeting on time and on point, ensuring that time is well spent.

If you're not willing to prepare for the event, then don't have it. Using the same agenda meeting after meeting is worse than having no agenda at all. It communicates to your team more clearly than you realize that you're running the ship on autopilot. Invest the time necessary to prepare for a useful meeting, and send the agenda out at least a day in advance so your team can prepare to participate, offer ideas, and engage. You expect them to speak intelligently about the topics so that decisions can be made in *this* meeting, so you must do the work ahead of time to equip them to do so. Everyone should be on the same mental page that says, "We're working to reduce the number of meetings. The best way to do this is to get things done while in this meeting."

Ask great questions of your team. And then let them talk. It's your job as a manager to ask great questions, ask your team for input, and then stop talking and listen. Your ratio of listening to talking should be 80/20. This means that instead of telling your employees what to do, you're asking them for feedback and helping them figure it out.

Set clear responsibilities. Be vividly clear in communicating your expectations for everyone as a result of the meeting. Ensure each person knows what they are responsible for doing. Do not leave a meeting without verbally letting everyone know what they are expected to do and deliver next.

Follow up on email. After each meeting, send a recap email detailing what was covered, the actions steps to be taken next, and who is responsible for taking them. I'm a big believer in the meeting recap email. Does it take time? Yes. Is it worth it? Yes. When I was an individual contributor, it helped reinforce what I had learned in meetings and reminded me of the tasks that had been assigned to me. When I prepared them as the leader, it helped reinforce the action steps for me, too. (I do the same thing with my *Learning Leader Show* podcast. I write my own detailed show notes after every episode. It helps me create faster recall and deeply reinforces what we talked about during the interview.)

There are some guidelines to writing a good recap email. Just sending someone the minutes, the actual transcript of the meeting, is typically not helpful. In my experience, the email won't get read. Even if your team does read it, they'll be trying to decipher what they are responsible for. Instead, I list what we spoke about in bullet points, making sure to highlight who is responsible for what, and any due dates that apply. It's even more effective if you add your own thoughts and takeaways, as well as moments of appreciation. I also include links to books or articles that we mentioned in the meeting to make it easy for my teammates to learn more. On that same note, having an assistant put together an email is not as effective because it lacks your input and voice.

You might be reading this and thinking, *Are you kidding me? Meetings already take too much of my time. This will cause them to take up even more.* Yes, that is correct. But remember, the purpose here isn't to reduce the amount of time devoted to meetings (although that will happen if you're being honest with yourself about whether a meeting is even needed in the first place). Rather, the goal is to greatly increase the *effectiveness* of the meetings you do have. To do that, there are no shortcuts, and extra work will be required of you as the team's leader. If you're going to have a meeting, you need to prepare, create an agenda, have direct action items, present a purpose for the meeting, and then close the loop afterward by making sure everyone knows the play and their responsibilities in executing it.

Leave the laptop behind. Leave your computer at your desk. Obviously, it is advantageous to draft more complete notes that precisely capture the content of the meeting and allow for a verbatim review of the material at a later date. Only it isn't. Research by Pam Mueller and Daniel Oppenheimer demonstrates that students who write their notes on paper learn more. Across three experiments, Mueller and Oppenheimer had students take notes in a classroom setting and then tested students on their memory for factual detail, their conceptual understanding of the material, and their ability to synthesize and generalize the information. Half of the students were instructed to take notes with a laptop, and the other half were instructed to write the notes by hand. As in other studies, students who used laptops took more notes. In each study, however, those who wrote their notes by hand had a stronger conceptual understanding and were more successful in applying and integrating the material than those who took notes with their laptops.[20]

People pay less attention to what is being said if they have electronics in front of them. Even the presence of a phone facedown on the table has a negative group effect on trust toward the owner of the phone. Instead, take notes the old-fashioned way: with a pen and a pad of paper, and leave your phone in your pocket. Also, in your one-on-one meetings with your team members, your phone should not be in sight. If you're constantly peeking at the computer or your phone, your conversation with your team member will suffer. In those moments, the person you are meeting with is the most important person. Your team members need to feel that, and you should give that to them if your goal is an open and honest dialogue. And move from behind your computer. I made a habit of moving my chair to the side of my desk to remove the obstacle (the desk) in our path to create a more open environment for speaking.

As the leader of the meeting, be prepared, be present, have a purpose, be engaged. One final tip: block off the 30 minutes prior to your meeting on your calendar and do not accept other meetings during that period. This ensures that you are punctual for your meeting, and it gives you time to prepare and change any minor parts of the agenda leading up to it. As the leader, your team looks to you to set the pace, and they will model their behavior after yours in their other meetings. When someone from your team earns a promotion and takes over a team of their own, they will likely pattern their meetings after how their boss always ran meetings. Give them an excellent example to follow.

KEY INSIGHTS

- Master the art of becoming an excellent communicator, verbally and in writing.
- We communicate to build relationships, express feelings, share ideas, and work together to accomplish what we cannot do on our own.
- Use the power of stories in your communication. Stories are how we think. They make information more memorable.
- Good listeners are like trampolines. They amplify, energize, and clarify your thinking as they are listening.
- Bad news does not get better with age. Despite your misgivings or fear, address issues quickly.
- High performers want feedback and will seek it out. Don't think your job is just to coach the low to mid-performers.
- Don't have meetings just out of tradition. Be very purposeful. *Why* are we having this meeting? Is it necessary? *What* is the goal of the meeting? *Who* needs to be in the room? *When* will it take place? Try 8 a.m. or 4 p.m. to avoid disrupting productive stretches of the day.

RECOMMENDED ACTIONS

- Write your story. Reflect on inflection points in your career. The act of recording them will help you better understand these moments. This will make you a better communicator when sharing them with others.
- Develop five potential questions you could ask team members as you MBWA (Manage By Wandering Around).
- Think of an important upcoming meeting and develop your specific meeting plan. Send an agenda to attendees in advance. Remember the why, what, who, and when priorities.
- Be on time. Start every meeting on time with no exceptions. People respect this and will learn to be on time due to your well-modeled behavior.
- Do not look at your phone or computer during a meeting. Put these devices away. Respect the others in the room by giving them your undivided attention.
- Block time on your calendar to regularly meet with high performers. Give candid feedback. Care personally and challenge directly.

6

MAKE THE GRADE

*It had long since come to my attention that people of
accomplishment rarely sat back and let things happen
to them. They went out and happened to things.*

—Leonardo da Vinci

When you raise your hand and step into the role of "the leader," you are making the choice (whether you are conscious of it or not) to be responsible for the results of your team. After embedding himself with New Zealand's All Blacks rugby team for a period of time, author James Kerr described to me the role of the leader as the person who "is responsible for the result, whatever that result is. And that sense of personal responsibility and ownership and accountability for that result—whichever way it goes: responsible if there's a win, but also equally responsible if things don't go to plan. Ownership and accountability and taking it on the chin, I think, is really fundamental. They're all kind of embroiled in that same knot of team and connection and authentic accountability."[1]

Being "responsible for the result" may sound simple enough. Most clichés do, in fact, and being accountable for results is certainly a well-worn cliché in leadership circles. But just because something is a cliché doesn't mean it ceases to be true. Yet there's a lot more to it than simply saying, "I'm responsible," and being the one who has to answer to others (a boss, a customer, a board, investors) for those results. Being accountable for your team's performance is a part of team leadership, but so too is the accountability you owe *to your team* to do the things that will help them achieve those results. Taking the blame or accepting the reward is simple and straightforward, even if it's not altogether *easy*. (If it was, blame-shifting and avoidance of accountability wouldn't be such a widespread leadership problem.) Affecting the outcome of the collective work of an organization or team is something else entirely. This side of leadership is much harder and far more complex, which is why it is done well so rarely.

RESULTS MATTER

Early in my career, I met with an executive from another company who had shown interest in hiring me for a significant leadership role. During that interview, he said to me, "I look for people who have had success in multiple life categories. I want leaders who've shown that they have the skill, will, and desire to 'figure it out,' regardless of the situation." Even though many years have passed since that meeting, I still remember his words with vivid clarity. I didn't end up taking the job that was offered, but that interview impacted me in a permanent fashion, nonetheless.

Excellent leaders get results. If the coach loses too many games, he gets fired. Regardless of the sport, this is a certainty. Likewise, in business: a leader who fails to produce results will soon find herself no longer leading her team. While I firmly believe in the virtue of focusing on the process to get there, it is vital that your record reflects a habit of actually "getting there."

Why? Organizations need to progress. They need to achieve revenue targets, to complete projects on time and within budget, and to create positive momentum moving forward. The responsibility for making that happen lies with the leader. Showing that you've done that in the past was likely key to earning that big promotion, and doing it now as the new leader is vital to *keeping your current role* and to setting yourself up for the next growth opportunity. How do you do that? In a nutshell: by understanding the role you play, understanding the tools you have at your disposal to help you, learning from your and others' experiences, and making the adjustments necessary to drive improvements.

"YOU HAVE TO DO ALL THREE"

When I landed the promotion that made me a manager for the first time, my initial plan was to stick to my natural strengths. I remember talking it over with my dad and telling him, "I'm more of an inspirational leader. I'll share vision and inspire the team to exceed our goals. I'm not really a numbers guy. I'll get someone else to help me with that." My dad didn't hesitate to stop that train of thought right in its tracks. "Don't ever say or think that again," he said. "You are running the team. You are now a leader. You must become a 'numbers guy' *and* continue to inspire. You need to lead, manage, *and* coach. To be excellent, *you have to do all three.*"

Looking back at my mindset is a bit embarrassing, frankly. I somehow got it into my head that I could be an excellent leader while only doing part of the job. Time proved my dad right, of course. Once I took on the responsibility of answering for the results of my team, I knew why: I couldn't fairly handle that responsibility if I wasn't willing to wear all three hats required of the role.

You may be asking yourself, "What's the difference between leading, managing, and coaching anyway? Is it just semantics?" There are many who say it is, including leaders I respect and admire like Tom Peters: "Leadership entails enormous responsibility. Management entails enormous responsibility. But my statement is silly, because there is no difference between the two."[2] Peters's expertise and view notwithstanding, I have found it helpful throughout my career to think of these three words as distinct functions, which overlap and intersect within the single role of being responsible for the performance of others, regardless of whether you call yourself a "leader," a "manager," or a "coach." And so, with apologies to Tom, that's how I will discuss them in this chapter.

Leading

"Leadership is at its best when the vision is strategic, the voice persuasive, and the results are tangible," writes Michael Useem.[3] The act of leading is about providing purpose, direction, and inspiration to the group. It presents a vision, sees the big picture, and devises a strategy to accomplish the mission at hand. In focusing on the communication of goals, building teams and coalitions, and seeking commitment from its members, the effect of leading on those members should be one of inspiration and empowerment. From Tom Peters:

> I believe that effective leadership—in a six-person accounting office, an elementary school, a computer factory, or a nation—is largely a function of the chief's vitality, willingness to empower others, and skill at exciting individuals about their own and their group's purposes.
>
> In business, the supreme strategist, who can dissect markets the way a chess master can evaluate his next five moves, is a precious commodity. But the chess master need only out-think his opponent. Once he decides to make a move, physically shifting the piece follows automatically.
>
> Not so for the leader of any organization. His or her rooks, knights, and pawns must be inspired—and then inspired all over again tomorrow—if world-class quality and continuous improvement are to be the everyday result.[4]

To lead well means to have what Robert Greene calls "a third eye"—a way of guiding you toward the larger picture while avoiding getting trapped in the hell of tactics. A great leader has an overriding sense of where she is taking the team at the macro level. "Most of us in life are tacticians, not strategists, writes Greene in his book, *The 33 Strategies of War*.[5] "We become so enmeshed in the conflicts we face that we can think only of how to get what we want in the battle we are currently facing. To think strategically is difficult and unnatural. You may imagine you are being strategic, but in all likelihood, you are merely being tactical."[6] Strategists think beyond a single battle or even a series of battles. They are focused on the playbook of the long game, in which they expect to survive multiple defeats and still push forward to victory. They don't fight just because the enemy army is present— they only fight when the time and location is right. Even then, they ask questions like *"Is it possible to gain victory without fighting this battle?"*

> To have the power that only strategy can bring, you must be able to elevate yourself above the battlefield, to focus on your long-term objectives, to craft an entire campaign, to get out of the reactive mode that so many battles in life lock you into. Keeping your overall goals in mind, it becomes much easier to decide when to fight and when to walk away.[7]

One of the biggest changes a manager goes through as they make the transition from individual contributor to leader is the necessary shift in mindset to thinking about the business from this higher-level perspective. As an individual contributor, you often only need to think of your goals, your actions, your work, your objective, at a singular level. When you get promoted, that all changes. You start thinking about company objectives, company mission, vision, and plans. And if you want to continue to progress, it's wise to start thinking about this as soon as possible. I did not learn this right away, but wish I had.

In order to lead like a strategic visionary, you must start by thinking like one. That means thinking through a progression of lenses, from the most high-level and general to ground-level and specific: from mission to vision to strategy to tactics.

This is our path to being a more strategic leader. Let's break it down.

Mission. *Why* do we do what we do? *Why* does our company exist? *Why* does THIS team (the one I am now leading) exist?

Vision. *Where* we are heading? It is the ultimate destination that connects the mission to our product, service, or goal, and therefore is necessarily aspirational in nature.

Strategy. This is the planning framework for *how* we will do the work of getting to the destination identified in our vision.

Tactics. The details of *what* must be done at an individual level to execute the plan. This is precisely what you are to do. The job function in specific detail. Given that, it should be collaborative, and the leader should empower the team in the planning process. And it must be vividly clear when rolled out. Ensure all questions are answered and the team is aligned and knows the plan. All tactics should be measurable and have ownership at the individual level.

. . . . .

A good system for thinking strategically and keeping that focus is to list your "Big 5" annual priorities. With such a list, you are positioned to plan how you will spend your time and effort working toward accomplishing these five. Here is an example of what that looks like, from my days leading a sales team:

1. **Supporting employees and customers.** Striving to be ever more intentional about taking care of the most important people to your team's success (your employees) and the second-most important people (your customers). Good intentions don't turn out to be much in the end unless and until they are channeled through well-designed systems aimed at operationalizing those noble ideas. Building those systems will take work.

2. **Maintaining the optimal level and mix of talent of your team.** This is all about recruiting, hiring, training, and coaching.

3. **Managing the metrics that matter.** What are the behaviors that truly lead to long-term sustained excellence on your team? Because "what gets measured gets managed," it's critical that

you know what matters most, have a way of measuring that, and then hold your team accountable for those results.

4. **Driving new account acquisition.** In business as in life, to live is to grow, and to grow is to live. Every company needs to continually acquire new customers if they are to grow.

5. **Keeping your current customers happy.** Counterintuitively, some of the biggest opportunities for growth lie with the happy clients you already have. Knowing how to identify those opportunities and convert them is vital. A bonus that comes from this key strategic focus are the insights you develop from regular contact with your actual customers (rather than just the reports of what your customers are doing). Whether or not you work in sales, a portion of your time should be spent on the front lines with the people who buy and use your product. Hear what they say about it: why they like it, what could be improved. Get their actual quotes. Feel their happiness and pain from what you offer. Gaining an understanding of how they actually speak will make you a better leader and better champion for your company. When giving a presentation, it's much more persuasive and impactful to use real quotes from real customers than to display a bunch of numbers on a screen. Learn their stories, and tell their stories. Get in the field and learn from firsthand experience.

Managing

Great management is figuring out how to work within the current constraints of the system you are in. It is the administration and stewardship of resources. It is because those resources are always limited—*always*—that the act of managing is even necessary. If time and money were truly of no consequence, then the very idea of a manager becomes irrelevant, for there are no decisions that need to be made: unlimited resources can be thrown at every project, and the work can take as long as it requires without consequence. In your new role as a manager, you will run into the hard limits of your resources—whether time, budget, or manpower—sooner than you would like. When you do, take heart. It is those limitations that make your new job a necessary one.

As a new manager, I was given a salary and variable compensation budget to work within (for the people I was to hire and work to retain). There was no negotiation, and I had no ability to request more money. That was what was budgeted and if the "superstar" candidate I desperately wanted demanded more money, I was out of luck. I had to find a way to make it work within those constraints. As a mid-level manager, this is part of the deal.

The same is true of the goals you will be accountable for leading your team to hit. Whether your team is charged with meeting targets on revenue growth, customer acquisition, product deployment, customer service success, or project management timelines, the dynamic will almost always feel the same: the constraints of aggressive goals, oftentimes set and dictated without your input.

When it came to the sales goals set annually for my team, if I felt they were unreasonable (an entirely common complaint among sales managers, regardless of industry), it didn't really matter. Those were the goals, and my job was to get our team to meet them, regardless of how unreasonable I felt they were. I learned to apply the advice my mom always gave me at times like this: "Don't worry about things that are out of your control. Only concern yourself with things where you can make an impact."

Resource constraints demand creativity. When you don't have the luxury of throwing more money or people at a problem, you must be able to step back, identify what it is you're trying to accomplish, and find a different way to do it. I would regularly request extra funds from various parts of the business for a "special contest" or anything to help inspire my team and get them excited. I worked in a multibillion-dollar business in which my team (in the grand scheme of things) represented a tiny fraction. I felt it was my job to seek out and find ways to show them love, compensate them with prizes, money, trophies, and great feedback when they worked hard and overachieved. But getting the extra money I asked for didn't always happen. In those situations, I had to come up with other ways to help my team feel rewarded and appreciated for their great performance.

I had a regular practice of sending emails to the senior leaders above me with a request for them. I'd ask them to send a *"great job!"* email to a member of my team that said something like: "Hey Jameson, I heard from Ryan that you are crushing it. One hundred eighty-nine percent of plan in April?! Wow, congratulations and thank you for your hard work!" Sometimes, I would draft the email for the senior leader because I knew how busy they were, and the last thing they wanted was another item on their massive to-do list. Invariably, the senior leaders were all too willing to oblige, especially when I made it easy for them to do good and look good doing it. Not a bad tradeoff for the few seconds it takes to copy what I wrote into their email, put my team member's email in the To: field, and hit send.

All of these little details are important, and they make a difference. All of us want to feel love and recognition when we've worked hard and done a great job. It is the manager's responsibility to make sure they feel that love when they've earned it, and to figure out creative ways to make that happen when your resources are limited.

Another type of resource that a great manager must learn how to make use of is the organization itself, and the network of possible partners it contains. Building allies and consensus around ideas and initiatives with other leaders in the business is one of the key aspects of being a manager that you don't think of as an individual contributor. Cultivating real relationships with other leaders who have nothing to do with your work, but may at some point in time is the necessary prep work for the task of leading through influence. You can't just go to these people when you need something from them. Doing so risks creating the opposite of a virtuous cycle: if you start to become known as someone who only interacts with others when you want something from them, the chances of them agreeing to help go down. On the other hand, if you have previously invested the time and effort into building a real relationship with someone, then when you need their assistance or their backing on an initiative, it is much more likely to happen. Do the planting work of building connections ahead of time with no specific goal in sight, and you'll be amazed at the generosity you will someday harvest when you most need it.

. . . . .

Managing limited resources is only one arena that requires the manager's attention. Another ubiquitous, but ever true cliché, vying for the manager's attention is "managing change." As your competitive business market never stops changing, so, too, will the ways your company conducts its affairs internally. As the leader of your team, your people will either experience these never-ending changes for the better or for the worse, depending on how you navigate them. When done well, how you manage change can serve as the steady bow of your team's ship, helping it cut through the turbulent waves of change while still staying on your prescribed course.

The primary reason change is met with resistance is uncertainty. No one likes uncertainty. If people lack confidence that their leaders really have a clear plan for where they're going, the chances that those changes are going to be implemented well and yield positive results are slim. Marcus Buckingham, author of *First, Break All the Rules,* says that it is this alleviation of uncertainty that makes leaders worth following: "You follow someone because they give you confidence in the future. 'I want to hitch my wagon to you.' The future can be scary and uncertain. A great leader finds a way of making the world less scary and bringing a level of certainty to a situation."[8]

One way to help your team navigate change successfully is to help them focus on *what isn't changing.* Many leaders try to implement change by highlighting the problems of the current state and contrasting that with the expected benefits of the new initiative. According to recent change management research highlighted in the *Harvard Business Review,* this rational approach may, in fact, be counterproductive:

Change leadership that emphasizes what is good about the envisioned change and bad about the current state of affairs typically fuels fears because it signals that changes will be fundamental and far-reaching. Counterintuitively, then, effective change leadership has to emphasize continuity—how what is central to 'who we are' as an organization will be preserved, despite the uncertainty and changes on the horizon.[9]

In other words, our manner of operation and our strategy may evolve, but our identity as a team will remain the same. All leaders who work in the corporate world have gone through changes and will go through more in the future. The only constant in business is that it changes. The most effective leaders are prepared for it, expect it, and understand how to communicate the mission to their team while it's happening. To overcome your team's resistance, intentionally couple your messages about the coming change with reassuring reinforcements of continuity.

One of the pioneers in leading change is bestselling author and Harvard professor John Kotter. In his book, *Leading Change*, he lays out an eight-stage process for guiding an organization through change. His process is one that I've referenced and used repeatedly over the course of my time leading teams:

1. Establish a sense of urgency.
2. Create the guiding coalition.
3. Develop a vision and a strategy.
4. Communicate the change vision.
5. Empower employees for broad-based action.
6. Generate short-term wins.
7. Consolidate gains and produce more change.
8. Anchor new approaches in the culture.

Here is an example of what that process looks and sounds like:

"This is happening within the next 60 days. Let's get in front of it and be early adopters and LEAD the way for the rest of our organization." At a high level, as leaders, it's imperative that we share the specifics about the timetable necessary to implement and make changes, thereby creating a sense of urgency. Next, we need to find the leaders within our team to be part of the guiding coalition. These people are the ones who understand that change is constant and see it as an *opportunity* to distinguish themselves among their peers. While others are worried about the unknown and uncertainty, these team leaders will *choose* to lead the way. They are the core of your guiding coalition.

Next, we must ensure our ability to communicate the story and the vision is clear, concise, memorable, and useful. It must be developed and shared effectively in order to impact the team in a positive way. Then give credit and empower your team. Grant them freedom. Trust them to make choices and decisions. This is not the time to microman-age and stand over their shoulder. When it's their decision, they will be more invested in achieving a positive result. Highlight and shine a bright light on the people who are embracing this. Create ways to celebrate and share the news of even small wins. Communicate the value of these wins to your team, especially to those who are still unsure. Finally, anchor these as part of the new behavioral norms and expectations.

Gene Kranz, NASA's flight director for the Apollo 11 and 13 missions, said, "Expecting high performance is a prerequisite to its achievement among those who work with you. Your high standards and optimistic anticipations will not guarantee a favorable outcome, but their absence will assuredly create the opposite."[10] The same is true for the expectations you have and communications about adopting change. This "new" way simply becomes "the" way. Document it. Share it. Say it. Do it.

Coaching

If leading is about strategic vision, and managing is about administra-tive stewardship, then coaching is about developmental teaching. To be a coach is to give instruction delivered not to educate or inform, but to *improve*. For the manager of a team, coaching in this manner falls into two types: coaching for professional development (performance) and coaching for personal development (growth).

Coaching for Performance

The best coaching for performance happens in the moments closest to when the performance happens. These regular, immediate bursts of micro-coaching should happen daily. Helping your team make the minor tweaks that improve their skill level doesn't require huge chunks of time devoted to training efforts. Rather, it is in the moments and minutes—both planned and unplanned—that may seem to those above you as inconsequential. Coaching that works in developing people's professional skills only comes from those who are competent at the craft. So, as the head coach of your team, you'd better know your stuff.

When I switched from leading a team that sold to lawyers to leading a team that sold to clinicians, the dramatic differences between the products and industries made for a humbling experience. I had to spend a lot of time learning the new industry, the verbiage of what was a veritable foreign language to me. But just because it was going to take time for me to learn the lay of the land in my new professional world, that didn't mean I could avoid engaging as my team's coach until that happened. While being mindful of what I didn't know and working diligently to close the gap, I was able to still offer micro-coaching moments that were industry agnostic, such as the fundamentals of communication skills in the context of business-to-business sales (how to open a meeting, follow-up questions that could have been asked, how to structure a proposal email, ways to secure the next appointment). These skills are as much a part of coaching moments for performance as is subject matter expertise.

Coaching for Development

Coaching for the personal development of your employees involves more long-term thinking. In this mode of teaching, your goal is to help them grow as a person in ways beyond their job performance. This requires having conversations about their career ambitions in a focused, one-on-one setting. Or sharing with them books, podcasts, or other tools for self-improvement aimed at their individual needs and strengths. These development conversations are a critical tool for creating the type of culture where people want to do their best work. When people know their boss has their long-term interests at heart, while also working on short-term ways to help them improve their work, the quality of their performance improves dramatically. In fact, if you embrace the concept of a leader doing both types of coaching, you'll be surprised at the new levels to which your people's "best" rises.

This requires a willingness to do the necessary hard tasks *and then go beyond* what most will do. That means making the effort to learn about each one of your direct reports in meaningful ways. What are they like as people? What are their interests outside of work? What is their individual motivation? Why do they work? What are their spouse's and kids' names? What could you do to assist them long term? How could you help them develop their career and prepare them for their next phase? How can you help them get promoted? How can you help them improve with a current project they are working on? What specific tweaks can you offer to help them improve as a performer? Answering these questions is critical to coaching your team well. And you can't answer these questions without getting to know your people and their work *really well.*

Believe it or not, there may be people in your organization who do not support you leading your team in this way. You may even have one of those people as your boss. I did, once. He disliked that I devoted so much time to the development portion of my coaching. He cared about short-term results and felt that my caring about the long-term excellence of the people on my team diverted time and energy away from generating those results. If you firmly believe as I do that it is our job as leaders to help our team members be successful long term, that "my success can only follow the success of my team," then you will have to create a plan for how to manage the resistance you may encounter from others. This is especially the case if the people you are helping to improve end up getting promoted to new jobs and leave your team, taking their production with them. Yes, that may cause you to have to answer to your boss, who just wants your team to keep hitting its number. But to that headache, I ask: Don't you want to be the leader who helps other people progress and grow? Being known as the manager who does that is something to be proud of and will ultimately help you in the long term more than any short-term result you can achieve.

Ask, Why Did You Win?

It's common for leadership teams to do a "root cause analysis" when something goes wrong. Something didn't work the way we wanted it to, so we need to learn why. Multiday summits are held in which the group comes together to deconstruct the failure and to analyze why something went wrong. And that's fine. But too often, managers in their coaching capacity operate the same way. In doing so, managers skip right over one of the first questions I always ask someone after they've achieved some levels of success: *why did you succeed?*

Failure analysis is valuable and should be done. However, the problem I've seen too often is not utilizing a form of after-action review following a *successful* outcome. It's understandable why: who wants to take the time away from celebrating a win and getting ready for the next challenge to dig into the analysis of the work we just did when it was successful? When you exceed your goals, metrics, or objectives, that is precisely the best time to take a moment to pause, reflect, and *understand why* it went well. Maybe you just got lucky? Then again, maybe not. As the leader, it is critical to know which one is right, and understand why something worked. You want to duplicate it, and you can't duplicate what you don't really understand. When I spoke with Michael Lombardi (former NFL general manager and winner of three Super Bowl rings), he shared a story about his time working with Bill Belichick, head coach of the New England Patriots. Most would argue that he's the greatest coach in professional football history. He's won six Super Bowls (and counting). Lombardi said, "Coach Belichick *always wanted to know why.* After a big win, we did more analysis than anything I've ever seen. We learned the intimate details of every single play to better understand *why* we won and how we could get even better. *That's* why he's won so much."

Here are some practical tips to help you do this.

Keep a Daily Diary

Knowing how you were feeling, why you made the decisions you made, in specific moments throughout the course of the year is critical in gaining an understanding of why something worked. Derek Sivers, entrepreneur (founder of CD Baby) and writer, shared why he believes it is important for us to utilize a daily diary:

> We so often make big decisions in life based on predictions of how we think we'll feel in the future, or what we'll want. Your past self is your best indicator of how you actually felt in similar situations. So it helps to have an accurate picture of your past. You can't trust distant memories, but you can trust your daily diary. It's the best indicator to your future self . . . of what was really going on in your life at this time. If you're feeling you don't have the time or it's not interesting enough; remember: You're doing this for your future self.[11]

Over the course of your career, you will thank yourself for keeping track of what was happening in the moments that preceded success. What were you thinking? What did you learn from your team? What did your boss say or do that had a positive or negative impact on you? By writing these down, you are connecting the dots that, in the future, you will be able to look back and connect into a picture of how your success was built.

Keeping a journal is also a fantastic tool for preserving the wisdom of perspective. Will Guidara, owner of New York's award-winning Eleven Madison Park restaurant, shared the fantastic advice his dad gave to him when he was young. "When you're a busboy, you have the perspective of a busboy. As soon as you become a waiter, you forever lose the perspective of a busboy. As soon as you become a manager, you forever lose the perspective of a waiter. My dad always made me journal, so that I could be the most empathetic leader that I could be one day because I would be able to actually go back and read my notes and have a greater capacity to connect with where the people I was leading were at in that moment."[12]

Interview Your Team

Don't wait for something to go wrong to have the deep conversations with members of your team. Analyze why they had a great year. Gather the commonalities among the top producers and performers on your team. *What do they actually do all day?* Approach each team member with a curious mind and a desire to learn about the business that each of them is running.

When I was managing my inside sales team, I would invite senior leaders of the business to sit with sales professionals on my team to watch and listen to how they operated. One particular sales professional on my team was the top producer in the entire division of the business. One of our C-suite leaders sat with him for an hour. Afterward, I said, "So, what did you learn?" He replied, "I was blown away by the mastery of this young professional and the speed at which he operated. He's created a system for himself to quickly do all of the administrative tasks of the job (emails, proposals, list creation to call, etc.). This allows him to speak to more prospective customers than the average person. He also has a great follow-up system in place so that nothing ever falls through the cracks, and he's on top of his entire deal flow."

The high-level leader then took what he learned from the sales rep on my team and shared it with others throughout the organization. This practice of studying and interviewing the top performing people can have lasting impact on both the employee and others. One, it helped other people at the company. Two, it shined a bright light on one of our best performers, thus branding him as not only a top performer but as someone whose methods could help others. That employee felt immense pride that his production and the way he achieved it could lead to the success of others. This multiplying effect had lasting positive impact on his career moving forward.

Interview Your Heroes

There is so much wisdom out there to be shared if you're willing to *ask*. In addition to regularly recording interviews for my podcast, *The Learning Leader Show*, with leaders from all walks of life (CEOs of large companies, entrepreneurs, Navy SEALs, professional athletes, coaches, bestselling authors), I have a regular practice of interviewing other people I look up to by email. I find the practice of asking someone—your favorite boss, a parent, or a leader in your community that has positively impacted people—to sit down and *write* their answers results in thoughtful and useful responses. Often, the person I'm "interviewing" in this way will *thank me* for "forcing" themselves to do that deep, introspective work. Some of my greatest learnings have come from doing this exercise on a regular basis.

Because of my positive experience with it, I've made this an assignment for the people I lead in my Learning Leader Circles and in my online course, The Learning Leader Academy. The feedback I receive from those I push to do this is often proof positive that my experience wasn't the rare exception. Here's what one participant shared with me: "Just received the answers back from my all-time favorite boss. The answers were incredible! It prompted a phone call, which then led to a meeting. I had not seen her in 10 years and now we've reconnected because of this exercise. Thank you!" So much good can happen from putting yourself out there and *asking* someone else what they think. It can reconnect you with past friends, colleagues, and mentors while putting you in the driver's seat of your learning. Make this part of your operating framework moving forward, and I promise you will not regret it. In fact, I would love to hear how this goes once you start doing this. Email me (Ryan@LearningLeader.com) after you've tried it, and let me know how it impacts you.

Training

Sales trainer and keynote speaker Phil Jones recently asked me: "Would you choose to be good, better, or at your best?" Without thinking, I instantly responded, "My best!"[13] That's the mistake nearly everybody in the world makes, Jones says. You have already outperformed what previously you would have called your best. We tell these lies to ourselves and say things like, "I tried my best." But if we honestly looked inside ourselves, we would realize we could have done better. We should all focus on continually getting better, not getting to the best. We will be in the chase of our best forever, knowing we'll never reach it. Practice and training are the exercises of that chase.

I learned through the grueling practices of Coach Ron Ullery the benefit of making practice harder than the games. We endured what felt like an endless degree of repetition to focus on perfecting the tiny details and most basic fundamentals. On top of being both physically and mentally better conditioned than every opponent we faced, we had also built up an amazing amount of muscle memory so that, by the time of the game, our bodies' execution had become nearly automatic. Legendary NFL coach Bill Walsh believed that mastering the basics was the best strategy for succeeding in pressure-packed situations: "I might do even less strategizing for a Super Bowl game, because in the midst of the extreme pressure I placed a premium on fundamentals."[14]

As a manager, I wanted our training sessions to make for a more challenging experience for my sales professionals than their actual sales calls. Training should be part of your weekly schedule. Some should be led by you (the manager), while others should be led by team members. Design an environment that is challenging while practicing, so that it creates a more "automatic" response and comes more easily when it's for real. As part of the training and practice regimen adopted by New Zealand's All Blacks rugby club, they focused on the Greek word *automatus,* which means "self-thinking."[15] Prepare so that your team creates performance instincts and does not have to "think" when they're on the field. Professional downhill skiers do this daily by "setting their edges" before racing down the mountain—a small but important maneuver to remind themselves of the tiny details they worked on in training.

As the manager of your team, it is up to you to cultivate an environment in which training (or practicing) becomes ingrained in the culture. During the interview with my dad for my 300th podcast episode, he said something that really captured the point about this:

> You can be at the top of your profession and still work on the tiny details of your craft every day. It's amazingly important. And if you can't take inspiration from that, then you just don't get it. I went to Japan one time on a trip and I got to visit a sales office, and I saw all over the office all these Japanese citizens who were salespeople there *practicing* the appointment they were about to go on over and over and over. How they're saying the words, how they're responding to objections, and I thought, *This is the way it's supposed to work.*

Sometimes, ensuring your team is properly trained means bringing in someone else to teach them. When a subject matter expert is required to help your team get better, it's your responsibility to find who could best fill that need and invite that person to speak to your team. If there is a new product rollout that would benefit your team to know more about, invite one of the key designers of that product to give a presentation and then listen to your team share what they've learned afterward. Develop a process in which they take what they learn, distill it to its essence, and explain it clearly and concisely. Create a consistent learning environment in which training and learning is just a part of the fabric of your team.

Jerzy Gregorek, world class weightlifter and creator of The Happy Body program, likes to say, "Hard choices, easy life. Easy choices, hard life."[16] It's much harder as the leader to create and deliver regular training. You will most likely receive pushback from members of the team.

That's OK. Doing the hard stuff now creates an easier life later. It's akin to the quote from legendary Navy SEAL Richard Marcinko, "The more you sweat in training, the less you bleed in combat."[17] It is much easier (and much more shortsighted) to say, "We don't have time for that. We have work to do." That's what most people do, and they miss opportunities to get better. To best set your team up for success, play the long game: train, train, train, and then practice, practice, practice.

THE FREEDOM OF HUMILITY

Joshua Becker, bestselling author of *The More of Less*, writes:

[Humility] grants enormous power to its owner. Humility offers its owner complete freedom from the desire to impress, be right, or get ahead. Frustrations and losses have less impact on a humble ego and a humble person confidently receives opportunity to grow, improve, and reject society's labels. A humble life results in contentment, patience, forgiveness, and compassion.[18]

I have chosen to close this chapter on getting results by focusing on what usually gets tossed overboard when positive results start rolling in: *humility*. It is often said that "Humility is not thinking less of yourself, but thinking of yourself less." In doing so, you free yourself to perform and help others do likewise without worrying about *you*. There is great power in leading with a service mindset that says it's *your job* to help other people be successful. Knowing this from the beginning is a good way to start. "The battle," Brian Koppelman told me, "is to accept who you are while not giving up on improving yourself. To continue to try to become the perfected version of you which you can never be. And to accept your own frailties and faults."[19]

For me to learn this, it took time, some maturity, and help from others. As a new, hard-charging, cold-calling new business sales professional, I looked out first for myself in my quest to get to and stay at the number one spot on the weekly stack rankings. As someone who got used to being at the top of those rankings, it was humbling (and at times, *humiliating*) to take over the team that was *dead last* in the rankings. All of a sudden, *my name* was attached to a team that was performing at 77 percent of plan. Nobody wanted to hear my excuses: "Well, I'm new and these aren't the people I hired," or, "I need some time to get us back on track." While those may have been true, I immediately became responsible for the results of my team the instant I become the manager.

Regardless of the new challenge ahead of you, the last course of action you should take is to separate yourself from the group because you are unhappy with the current results. Trust me when I say this: the best way to avoid doing that is to make humility a central piece of your mental leadership software. When you take the posture that it isn't about *you*, then you can avoid doing things to save face and get down to doing the messy work of helping your team excel. I urge you not to make the same mistakes that I have made and to learn this earlier in your career. It will serve you (and the people you lead) much better. As investment CEO Brent Beshore told me, thinking of life in a serving versus served mentality, "The more I give with no expectation of reciprocity, the better life goes. For others and for me. [It's] counterintuitive and countercultural."[20]

I asked one of my favorite (and most effective) bosses, Dustyn Kim, about her ability and willingness to say the words "I don't know" and to regularly share her fears and vulnerabilities with her team (I was a director at the time, and every member of our team was that level or higher). This is what Dustyn told me in response:

> This approach is definitely a natural instinct for me. Having said that, I had moments when I transitioned to a larger general manager role where I questioned that instinct. I wondered if I would be respected by the team if I didn't always have a clear path and most, if not all, of the answers. As I grappled with that, I realized it wasn't going to work for me for the following reasons:

1. I'm not that good of an actor/wasn't sure I could pretend
    to have all the answers;
2. It would lead to me putting a lot of pressure on myself,
    and given my high personal standards, would likely lead
    to me feeling like I was constantly failing; and
3. Most importantly, I realized that some of the best answers
    to our challenges were likely to come from the team (both
    my direct reports and the broader team that was in front
    of the prospects and customers all day every day).

Plus, I knew that if you all felt involved in crafting our path forward you would be more likely to support it and engage in a more
meaningful way. It was really scary at first to be that exposed on
such a grand scale (e.g., being mic'd up with lights shining on you
as you look out at a huge audience of people that you need to lead
and inspire), but once I tried it, the positive feedback loop that
resulted told me I was on the right path.

Dustyn never once used the word *humility*. Fitting, because that's
exactly what leading with humility looks like.

MANAGING UP

What do you do, though, when the people you are responsible for delivering results to aren't examples of humble leadership like Dustyn? One
of the most common emails I receive from listeners of *The Learning
Leader Show* goes something like this: "Ryan, I am all about personal
and professional development. I read books, watch TED talks, listen to
your podcast. I'm always trying to learn more and improve. However,
I work for a boss (or bosses) who don't show any of the same curiosity
that I do. *They have the mentality that they've got it all figured out.* And
I've found that while they are decent people, they definitely don't have
it all figured out. . . . What should I do?"

Managing your boss (and your boss's boss, etc.) is a challenge, and yet it's a skill that can be developed. If you choose to work in an organization where you have a boss, remember that part of your role is to *make their life easier.* Regardless of their mindset toward growth and any other disagreement you may have, if you want to remain working for your current company (and that boss), then you should be focused on two things: (1) serving the people you lead, and (2) helping your boss be successful.

Often, it is easy to judge the boss or CEO as being a bad leader. We've all done it. From our point of view, there are obviously things that we would be doing if we had that job. But therein lies the issue. We are looking at it from *our* point of view, not *theirs.* Be careful to judge someone too quickly when you don't have the full picture. We are all imperfect—just in different ways.

The most important aspect for us to learn and decode regarding leaders whom we find lacking is their intentions. Do they have positive intentions, wanting to do the right thing? If yes, then chances are their ability to effectively lead is being hamstrung by a lack of knowledge, skill, and/or experience. If that's the case, *we can work with that.* We can offer ideas. We can, carefully, pick our spots to "coach upward." We can share with them how we feel when they act in a certain way that causes problems for us and others (because odds are you're not the only one feeling the negative effects of ineffectual leadership). In short, we can find ways to work with good people who do bad things because, as good people, they are likely able and open to taking constructive feedback that is given in a positive fashion. As Hall of Fame coach John Calipari told me onstage at an event at the 2019 NCAA Final Four, "You can have a bad deal with good people. Stuff happens. But you can never have a good deal with bad people."

If, on the other hand, you determine that this leader is acting in a willfully negative fashion, not caring how their behavior impacts you and your team, then you have some hard decisions to make. In that situation, it may be time to take the long-term view and start looking outside of your current organization for opportunities to grow your career. Take great care in studying the situation and the leader you have concerns about. You must ultimately decide what is the truth about the person and choose your response accordingly: (a) stay and coach, give feedback, and speak honestly, or (b) get your résumé together and begin your search for an organization that is a better fit for you. This is not a choice to make lightly because it is not a decision you want to get wrong.

One key point to remember: it is important that you don't show your frustrations with your boss to the team that you are leading. As leaders, we have a responsibility to bring optimism and enthusiasm to our team. We cannot allow ourselves to take the easy path of dumping on the boss in front of them as this will not help them to be their best. Doing so will only drag them down into a valley of frustration as well.

One of the best ways you can coach or manage up is to build the culture and habits you want to see on your own team, generate winning results from it, and watch it spread. Let your results preach the gospel of leadership that is humble, management that is creative, and coaching that trains hard. Build it from within and watch it spread. This is a long-game play. It takes time and requires high performance on your team. Soon enough, other groups in the organization will be asking you how you did it, what you did, why you did it, and how they can do it, too—developments that can convert even the most skeptical of bosses to your cause.

KEY INSIGHTS

- We must lead, manage, *and* coach.
- The leader is responsible for the results of the team, whatever those results may be.
- Leading provides purpose, direction, and inspiration. A leader presents a vision, sees the big picture, and devises a strategy to accomplish the mission.
- Managing is figuring out how to work within the current constraints of the system you are in (e.g., money, people, systems).
- Managing change is a regular duty. The alleviation of uncertainty makes leaders worth following.
- Coaching is about developmental teaching. It is instruction to improve. We coach for performance and for developmental growth.
- Your success as a leader will only follow the success of your team.
- Humility is not thinking less of yourself, but thinking of yourself less. It frees you to perform without the desire to impress, be right, or get ahead.
- Lead with a service mindset. It's your job to help other people be successful.

RECOMMENDED ACTIONS

- List your big five annual priorities. This will position you to plan how best to spend your time and effort.
- Detail the notable constraints that you must "manage around" in your business.
- Do a postmortem, after-action review after every project. Learning from success is equally important as learning from failure. When you win or lose, you need to know *why*.
- Think of the best coaching that you have ever received. Detail the elements that made it great.

CONCLUSION: THE PAYOFF

The word *arete* means "excellence of any kind" or "moral virtue."[1] In early Greek, this meaning was related to the idea of the fulfillment of purpose or function, the act of living up to one's full potential.

. . . . .

"Great leadership is about solving problems. Run toward the problems, and work to solve them. Don't fixate on getting promoted. Focus your attention on doing great at your current job. And then doors will open." That's how Carly Fiorina described leadership to me. "You need an equal measure of optimism with realism. You must see the current state as it is. It's important to believe things will get better (optimism), but also be clear-eyed and realistic. Be honest. See truth, and act on it."[2] For Fiorina, this perspective is what carried her from her first entry-level role to the top job as CEO at tech pioneer Hewlett-Packard (becoming the first female CEO of a Fortune 50 company in the process) and ultimately to running for the White House as a candidate for president in 2016.

It is also a great way to describe the fundamental ethos that is the foundation of this book. Leaders—the ones worth following—are those who see themselves, their team, and the challenges before them with an unvarnished honesty. They are intentionally aware of the gaps, shortcomings, and blind spots. They see reality, but they don't accept it as destiny. Instead, they set to work to fill in those gaps, overcome those shortcomings, and illuminate the blind spots. Leaders undertake these efforts in the belief that improvement of themselves and their team is not only possible but *inevitable* if one follows the process, embraces learning with humility, and inspires others to do the same. To lead in this fashion is not to seek glory or benefit for oneself; rather, it is to use the power that comes from that position to clear the road of obstacles so that others can pursue their own success unhindered. Do this, and the feeling you will experience as a leader who leads well and sees the success of those you've helped is a unique brand of pure joy.

. . . . .

It had been about five years since Jennifer had come into my office and destroyed my preconceived notions of what being a manager meant within my first week on the job. It was February, and our company's entire sales force and executive leadership had gathered in Dallas, Texas, for our national sales meeting. The last night of the event was the Circle of Excellence awards dinner. My team had just wrapped up a big year, and this celebration was the culmination. Whether our performance had been good enough to win Team of the Year remained to be seen, but the preliminary numbers had us hopeful.

As the dinner concluded, the party started to crank up with loud music and a vibrant light show. Then came time for the announcement of the winners: the sales professionals and teams who had outperformed their goals to such an extent that they joined the Circle of Excellence. About halfway through the list, I heard my name, and our team's table erupted in celebration and hugs. We had done it. It had been a long, hard climb from the team that was dead last and only 77 percent to plan a few years before. We had gone through big changes, both in culture and in the makeup of the team. Though they had been hard, those changes had culminated in this moment. To experience the thrill of dramatic improvement was proof positive that implementing a mindset of curiosity, empowerment, and growth was the key to exceeding the stretch goals put in front of us by our company. That feeling of representing my team, and us finishing at the top of the stack rankings, was as gratifying a moment as I've ever had in my career.

Following the celebration, I was asked to interview for a director role with bigger, general management responsibilities. At the end of the process, I was offered the job, and my new boss simply said, "Do exactly what you did with your team, but now do it on a larger scale. That's all I ask." That promotion wasn't something I had set out to chase when

I started my management journey. It was the reward for excellence in taking care of the responsibilities right in front of me. As it was with me, I am confident it will be with you, too: being focused on being *great at your current role* will lead to opportunities to grow in your career in the future.

> *You never conquer a mountain. You stand on the summit for a*
> *few brief minutes, and then the wind blows your footsteps away.*
> —ARLENE BLUM

. . . . .

As a new manager, having a "general dissatisfaction with your current skill set" (that's how Zvi Band, CEO of Contactually, describes it)[3] will create a mindset to stretch yourself. To learn. To grow. Through discipline, you can build the habits that are foundational to a mode of constantly consuming new information. Then test your learnings in a real environment to understand what works for you and, most important, *why*. Spend a few moments each day reflecting on your experiments and taking inventory of what insights should remain as part of your ever-evolving way of operating. Then put yourself in situations to share your findings and learnings with others. Do this, and in six months you'll look back and be amazed at the level of growth that's occurred in yourself. It will motivate you to continue along that path.

I love the way NBA star J. J. Redick puts it: "You've never arrived. You're always becoming."[4] Redick has had plenty of opportunities to believe he had "arrived": a McDonald's High School All American, he was twice a consensus first-team All-American and named the National Player of the Year as a senior at Duke University in 2006. Following his sterling career at college basketball's preeminent program, Redick realized his dream of making it to the NBA when he was drafted in the first round by the Orlando Magic in 2006.

He is often asked to speak to audiences, ranging from college basketball teams to the executives and leaders of Fortune 500 companies. At one such event, Redick noticed that a player he was speaking to had a tattoo on his body that said "ARRIVED." The message of the tattoo stuck with Redick ever since. J.J. completed his thirteenth season with the Philadelphia 76ers, his best statistical year of his career, and then signed a two-year, $26.5-million contract at the age of 35. An unheard-of-sized contract for an undersized player of that age in the NBA. He defines what it means to continually improve on a daily basis.

For Redick, his focus is on continuous progress and improvement. It's about climbing the mountain and never reaching the summit, and yet still enjoying the climb. By trusting the process and doing the work necessary for daily improvement, you will experience the beneficial effects of aggregating even marginal, seemingly unseen gains. Don't ever think that you've arrived. Foster the mindset that you're always becoming.

Strive to lead in a manner in which you are constantly *expanding the edges of your competency*. Be thoughtful and intentional about how you expand those edges. Sign up for an improv class, learn to play guitar, learn a second language, take a class on a topic you know nothing about, learn to paint, travel to a country where they don't speak your language. We don't know what we're capable of until we are forced to do it. You should be expanding your zone of competence on a daily basis, and not just in the realm of being a great leader for your team. Take this same approach to life. Strive for incremental gain. But only *if* you care about excellence. Only *if* you care to get better. Only *if* you believe that you have the capacity to improve. I know you do, but that doesn't matter. The real question is: *Do you?*

ACKNOWLEDGMENTS

"A book," as my friend Chris Fussell says, "is more than words on paper. It's a complex project between people." This book could not have happened without the help of a group of remarkable people. I have drawn from my 350-plus podcast interviews, casual one-on-one conversations among friends, peers, coworkers, email interviews, moments in the huddle, on the sideline, in the weight room, and with the great leaders and coaches whom I've been fortunate to play for and with.

My editor, Casey Ebro at McGraw-Hill: After our initial 90-minute phone conversation, I thought, *Casey gets it. She will be the perfect partner for this.* Thank you for believing in my ability to share what the Learning Leader message is all about. Your guidance, support, and feedback have made this book infinitely better than it would have been without you.

Lance Salyers: Without you, this book would not have happened. You've been a partner in clarifying my thoughts and words from our early informal conversations at LexisNexis to our idea sessions and Slack chats throughout the writing process. Your ability to visualize the story, use metaphors, and edit my rough first drafts made this book what it is. Thank you.

Jim Levine: A few years ago, I started asking each podcast guest, "Who is the best literary agent in the world?" Your name kept coming up, both from your clients and from those who have worked with other literary agents. Thank you for believing in me, my proposal, and the potential of this book.

Sara Stibitz: For taking my rough ideas and helping turn them into a great proposal that Casey (and McGraw-Hill) wanted to buy, thank you!

To the best bosses I've ever worked for:

Rex Caswell: I learned the value of taking care of your people and performance metrics from you.

Bryan Miller: I learned about the importance of great storytelling and of being someone who could walk the talk from you.

Dustyn Kim: I learned strategy, vulnerability, and toughness from you. I appreciate your willingness to be open about the struggles of being a high-performing working mom. You've inspired me and many others in a big way.

Sean Fitzpatrick: You promoted a "sales guy" to a very different strategic role with greater responsibility, and you saw more value in me than I saw in myself at the time. Thank you.

Sean Hough: You are a pure grinder who worked his way to big roles and led successfully. I admire that.

Scott Schlesner: A genuine family man who loves hard and showed that nice guys win on a regular basis.

Lee Rivas: A long-term mentor who gave practical guidance for many years. Thank you.

Ron Ullery and Bob Gregg: You believed in a skinny eighth grader who had no clue what he was doing, and you had the guts to name him your starting quarterback as a freshman. Your willingness to push took me to levels of performance and leadership that I did not think I was capable of. I owe my college scholarship to both of you. I learned the value of discipline, hard work, preparation, and resilience from watching you and being coached by you. Other than my parents, the most fortunate aspect of my upbringing is that I got to play for you both.

My former teammates: Tony Abboud, Josh Betts, Sam Block, Ralph Bracamonte, Matt Brandt, Dan Braner, Andy Capper, Luke Clemens, Brad Colson, Andy DeVito, Zac Elcess, Austen Everson, Brandon Godsey, Jason Griffith, Anthony Hackett, A. J. Hawk, Phil Hawk, Brandon Hiatt, Alphonso Hodge, Ray Huston, Dontrell Jackson, Terrell Jones, Mike Larkin, Steve Lawrence, Ahmona Maxwell, Scott Mayle, Willy McClain, Matt Muncy, Adam Newton, Mike Nugent, Stafford Owens, Marquis Parham, Adam Porter, Matt Pusateri, Fred Ray, Ben

Roethlisberger, Tyler Russ, Scott Sagehorn, Joe Serina, Spencer Shrader, Rob Stover, Spencer Tatum, Adam Taylor, Dennis Thompson, Brent Ullery, J. D. Vonderheide, Brian Westerfield, Jon Zimmerman, and so many more. Thank you for teaching me how to work, prepare, and win.

Doug Meyer: Without you, much of the world that has opened up to me would not have done so. No book, no leadership advisory, nothing. *The Learning Leader Show* would be just a podcast, a hobby, and a side hustle. Your vision made it a reality and a real business. Thank you for your support, your friendship, your mentorship, your guidance, and the care you have for my entire family. I'm inspired by your love for Kersten, Jacob, and Jocelyn. Your actions inspire me to be a better husband, dad, and leader.

Dave Brixey: Your support, care, and pride in my work and how it supports the firm means so much to me. Thank you for being there when I need you and always having my back.

Brixey & Meyer team members: Thank you for welcoming me with open arms. It is an absolute joy for me to come to work every day, and that is because of you. These past two years working together have flown by, and it's only the beginning. I'm so excited for what's next.

My former team members: I'd love to name you all, but it would take another book.

Jameson Hartke and Parker Mays: I'm inspired and honored by your growth from being my mentees to now being my peers. I've learned so much from you about competing, pushing yourself beyond what you think you're capable of, and sustaining excellence. I'm happy and lucky to call you friends.

John Mers, David George, and Dave Campbell: You were the initial hires I was so lucky to make on the original Team Hawk. Without you, our team culture never would have developed. Your willingness to help others while simultaneously being excellent at exceeding your individual goals was exceptional. Thank you.

Brent Scherz: I admire your work ethic, desire to continuously improve, and how quickly you've been able to learn and develop new skills.

John Bierley, Monica Brewer, Aaron Campbell, Kevin Clark, David Daoud, Monica Deal, Trip Duncan, Laura Gaddis, Amanda Geddie, Chris Gerspacher, Matt Hein, Marian Langley, Bill McKinley, Tom Ogburn, Tom Osif, Erin Shelby, Karan Singh, Laura Smith, Reinaldo Smith, Paul Speca, Kyle Williams, Carolyn Young, and all of the incredible people at LexisNexis: Thank you.

Scott Cable, Drew Callahan, Scott Dovner, Dave Dwyer, Amanda Gianino, Marc Gluckman, Michelle Marchant, Brandon McCune, Therese Mugge, Guyan Randall, David Shelby, Kimberly Shepley, Mandi Siller, and so many others from that great Elsevier team: I appreciate how you welcomed me at the beginning and have stayed in touch since I left the company.

Bryan Wish: I've loved working on this project with you and having regular idea-creation sessions. I admire your willingness to work and connect with others. Thank you.

Jeremy Office: Thank you for coming to my keynote in South Florida and offering such caring feedback. The deep, vulnerable conversation we had over dinner helped me more than you realize. That's when I learned what *Ancora imparo* is all about. Thank you. Good to see a fellow Centerville Elk out on the road. You made that time away from my family feel like home.

Greg Meredith: I will always remember that day as we waited in line at Chipotle, you turning to me and saying, "You know, you should start a podcast. I think you would be really good at it. You have the combination of the interviewing experience and the ability to sell." That was over six years ago. I value your mentorship, guidance, friendship, and your willingness (and ability) to think differently from the crowd. It inspires me.

Charlie McMahan: I treasure our one-on-one talks. Thank you for your belief in me and for being so giving of your knowledge. Your words and actions have had a significant impact on my life.

Jeff (JD) Kennard: I finished this manuscript the week that you passed away. You remain one of my all-time favorite teammates, friends, and human beings. Your ability to see people, understand them, and help them was beyond that of any person I've known. You were perhaps the most self-aware person I've ever met. So much of what is written in this book comes from my time as your teammate (11 years on the same team!). Thank you, and I miss you. Your wife, Kate, is an absolute champion and warrior. Rest assured, we are all committed to supporting her and your boys, Cooper and Christian.

The members of my leadership circles: Neil Anderson, Josh Ballantine, Nicci Bosco, Terry Brown, Jacob Crawford, Nick DiNardo, Jeff Estill, Matthew Evetts, Tony Hixon, Kaitlyn Jordan, Rebecca Jutkus, Matt Kaminski, Keegan Linza, Parker Mays, Lizzie Merritt, Ben Miller, Tony Miltenberger, Joe Neikirk, Larry Seiler, Kylie Sobota, Betsy Westhafer, Derek Williams: One of the most rewarding aspects of my work is the regular time I get to spend meeting with all of you. You are all growth-oriented, highly motivated, super intelligent people. We've bonded over the common theme of being "learning leaders," and I'm so happy that we have. I'm fortunate to facilitate these conversations and look forward to them.

My podcast guests: Too many to name all, but your willingness to invest hours recording with me have been some of the greatest learning moments of my life. Some of the more notable ones who have been so helpful: Mitch Albom, Scott Belsky, Brent Beshore, Jay Bilas, Liv Boeree, Chris Borland, Marcus Buckingham, David Burkus, Susan Cain, Ryan Caldbeck, James Clear, Henry Cloud, Derek Coburn, Kat Cole, Joey Coleman, Jim Collins, Beth Comstock, Bill Curry, Annie Duke, Ryan Estis, David Epstein, Tasha Eurich, Carly Fiorina, Chris Fussell, Jayson Gaignard, Scott Galloway, Allen Gannett, Seth Godin, Adam Grant, Robert Greene, Verne Harnish, Dan Heath, Clay Hebert, Todd Henry, Todd Herman, Ryan Holiday, Alex Hutchinson (for helping me rewrite the first story in this book), Chase Jarvis, Phil Jones, James Kerr, Tim Kight, Maria Konnikova, Brian Koppelman, Pat Lencioni, Alison Levine, Michael Lombardi, David Marquet, Dave Matthews, Philip McKernan, Charlie McMahan, Stanley McChrystal (for the incredible trip to Gettysburg and for writing the Foreword to this book!), Cal Newport, Neil Pasricha, Tom Peters, Dan Pink, Brady Quinn, George Raveling,

J. J. Redick, Sarah Robb O'Hagan, Gretchen Rubin, Adam Savage, Brian Scudamore, Simon Sinek, Shane Snow, Jim Tressel, Tim Urban, Mike Useem, Vanessa Van Edwards, Gary Vaynerchuk, Jenny Vrentas, Todd Wagner (for the dinner that started this all), Liz Wiseman (for the title of this book!), and so many more. Being able to continue our dialogue as we progress and develop real friendships wildly exceeds any expectations I had ever set. It's surreal to become friends with your heroes. Thank you for continuing to enrich my life and be there for me.

Listeners of *The Learning Leader Show*: Thank you for your overwhelming support, feedback, and positive reinforcement on a regular basis. The in-person comments, emails, social media posts, etc. are fuel for me and continue to drive my passion to follow my curiosity and obsessions with great rigor. I am fascinated by deep conversations with interesting people. Your support gives me the opportunity to do what I love on a daily basis. Thank you.

Mom: Thank you for being true to yourself and always telling it exactly like it is to me and to everyone else. People always know where they stand with you, and I love that. It takes courage and inspires me. I hit the mother lottery with you, and I'm so grateful. On top of that, you are the most loving Mimi to all of your grandkids, and they love you more than anything. Thank you.

Pistol: You are the model for what a great leader should be—optimistic, always believing that things will go well, treating every day as a holiday, and always choosing to be kind to others. Without you, none of our family's success happens. No pro football, no books, no scholarships, nothing. I will forever try to live up to the example you set, fully knowing that it's not possible to match. Thank you for setting the standard for what it means to be an excellent husband, dad, and leader.

Matt (Berk): Since the day Nathan was born, I've studied and learned from your actions, which have shown me how to be a great dad. I aspire to developing the same skills you have with your hands and with building things (but I know I will never be as good as you). Most of all, thank you for your unyielding support from day one. I know it's never wavered and never will.

AJ: I have looked up to you for a long time. Your dedication to consistently work insanely hard has inspired me from a young age. The key to your success is your willingness to show up every day and work, and that inspires me. The humility with which you carry yourself, despite your immense success, is almost hard to believe, yet I get to see it daily. I'm so proud of you, and I'm lucky that you are my brother.

Brooklyn, Ella, Addison, Payton, Charlie: I love you so much. I am incredibly proud of the people you are becoming. When we meet with your teachers and hear that you've helped others, that you choose kindness, and that you work hard, it makes us so proud. Thank you for being the inspiration behind all the work that we do.

Miranda: Your love and support are beyond words. It's no surprise that my greatest achievements started happening when you came into my life. Your magnetic personality, your beauty, your intelligence, your work ethic are beyond measure. And you're the toughest person I've ever met. Thank you for choosing to be with me, and consciously making that choice again every single day. I love you.

NOTES

Introduction

1. Ovans, Andrea. "Overcoming the Peter Principle." *Harvard Business Review.* December 22, 2014. https://hbr.org/2014/12/overcoming-the-peter-principle (accessed July 25, 2018).

Chapter 1

1. Eurich, Tasha. "What Self-Awareness Really Is (and How to Cultivate It)." *Harvard Business Review.* January 4, 2018. https://hbr.org/2018/01/what-self-awareness-really-is-and-how-to-cultivate-it (accessed February 7, 2019).
2. Eurich, Tasha. Interview with Ryan Hawk. *The Learning Leader Show,* "Episode 204: Dr. Tasha Eurich—How to Become More Self-Aware." Podcast audio. May 14, 2017. https://learningleader.com/tashaeurich/.
3. Id.
4. Colvin, Geoff. *Talent Is Overrated.* Boston: Nicholas Brealey Publishing, 2008. (Kindle version, p.117.)
5. https://www.hoganassessments.com/assessment/hogan-personality-inventory/.
6. http://www.hexaco.org/.
7. https://www.gallupstrengthscenter.com/home/en-us/strengthsfinder.
8. Grant, Adam. "Goodbye to MBTI, the Fad That Won't Die." *Psychology Today.* September 18, 2013. https://www.psychologytoday.com/us/blog/give-and-take/201309/goodbye-mbti-the-fad-won-t-die (accessed February 11, 2019).
9. Kashdan, Todd B., and Paul J. Silvia. "Curiosity and Interest: The Benefits of Thriving on Novelty and Challenge." ResearchGate. January 2009. https://www.researchgate.net/profile/Todd_Kashdan/publication/232709031_Curiosity_and_Interest_The_Benefits_of_Thriving_on_Novelty_and_Challenge/links/09e41508d50c5af6d3000000.pdf (accessed July 25, 2018).
10. Id.
11. Kaufman, Scott Barry. "Schools Are Missing What Matters About Learning." *The Atlantic.* July 24, 2017. https://www.theatlantic.com/education/archive/2017/07/the-underrated-gift-of-curiosity/534573/.
12. Munger, Charlie. "USC Law Commencement Speech." Genius.com. https://genius.com/Charlie-munger-usc-law-commencement-speech-annotated (accessed January 18, 2019).
13. Useem, Michael. *The Leadership Moment: Nine True Stories of Triumph and Disaster and Their Lessons for Us All.* New York City: Crown Business, 1999.

14. Useem, Michael. Interview with Ryan Hawk. *The Learning Leader Show*, "Episode #298: Michael Useem—How to Become a Learning Machine." Podcast audio. February 17, 2019. https://learningleader.com/useemhawk298/.

15. Useem. *The Leadership Moment*, at 149 (Kindle ed.).

16. Navarro, Joe. Interview with Ryan Hawk. *The Learning Leader Show*, "Episode 275: Joe Navarro—The World's #1 Body Language Expert (FBI Special Agent)." Podcast audio. September 22, 2018. http://learningleader.com/joenavarroryanhawk/.

17. Schwartz, Katrina. "Don't Leave Learning Up to Chance: Framing and Reflection." KQED.org. https://www.kqed.org/mindshift/46316/dont-leave-learning-up -to-chance-framing-and-reflection (accessed January 20, 2019).

18. Scott, Kim Malone. Interview with Ryan Hawk. *The Learning Leader Show*, "Episode 223: Kim Malone Scott—Using Radical Candor to Be a Great Boss." Podcast audio. September 17, 2017. http://learningleader.com/episode-223-kim-malone -scott-using-radical-candor-great-boss/.

19. Beshore, Brent. Interview with Ryan Hawk. *The Learning Leader Show*, "Episode #293: Brent Beshore—How to Get Rich Slow & Live an Optimal Life" Podcast audio. January 12, 2019. https://learningleader.com/beshorehawk/.

20. Raveling, George. Interview with Ryan Hawk. *The Learning Leader Show*, Episode #281: George Raveling—Eight Decades of Wisdom: From Dr. Martin Luther King to Michael Jordan. Podcast audio. October 27, 2018, https://learningleader.com/ ?s=george+raveling.

21. Elkins, Kathleen, "Buffett's Partner Charlie Munger Says the Key to Wisdom Is a Habit Anyone Can Form." CNBC.com. https://www.cnbc.com/2017/08/21 /buffetts-partner-charlie-munger-share-the-key-to-wisdom.html (accessed January 22, 2019).

22. "Reading 'Can Help Reduce Stress.'" *The Telegraph*. March 30, 2009. https://www .telegraph.co.uk/news/health/news/5070874/Reading-can-help-reduce-stress.html.

23. Pack, Lauren. "Jury Issues Death Decree for Man Convicted of Killing Fairfield Attorney and a Witness." *Dayton Daily News*. October 23, 2010. https://www .daytondailynews.com/news/local/jury-issues-death-decree-for-man-convicted -killing-fairfield-attorney-and-witness/xccUYfEf1mraeGtweHdHWP/ (accessed January 24, 2019).

24. *Evil Twins*. "Do No Harm." Season 4, Episode 3. Produced by Cat Demaree and Matthew Warshauer. Investigation Discovery. October 29, 2015.

25. Herman, Todd. Interview with Ryan Hawk. *The Learning Leader Show*, "Episode #295: Todd Herman—Using Alter Egos to Transform Your Life." Podcast audio. January 27, 2019. http://learningleader.com/toddhermanryanhawk/.

26. Gladwell, Malcolm. *Outliers*. Penguin, 2009.

27. Ericsson, Anders. Interview with Ryan Hawk. *The Learning Leader Show*, "Episode 147: Anders Ericsson—What Malcolm Gladwell Got Wrong About the 10,000 Hour Rule." Podcast audio. August 3, 2016. http://learningleader.com /episode-147-anders-ericsson/.

28. Colvin, Geoff. *Talent Is Overrated*. Boston: Nicholas Brealey Publishing, 2008. (Kindle version, p. 66.)
29. Tolisano, Silvia. "Amplify Reflection." *Langwitches: The Magic of Learning* (blog). August 20, 2016. http://langwitches.org/blog/2016/08/30/amplify-reflection/ (accessed February 5, 2019).
30. "Confucuis Quotes." BrainyQuote.com. https://www.brainyquote.com/quotes /confucius_136802 (accessed February 6, 2019).
31. "docendo discimus." Merriam-Webster.com. https://www.merriam-webster.com /dictionary/docendo%20discimus (accessed February 6, 2019).
32. "Self-Explanation," LearnLab.org. https://www.learnlab.org/research/wiki/index .php/Self-explanation (accessed February 6, 2019).
33. Jarrett, Christian. "Self-Explanation Is a Powerful Learning Technique, According to Meta-analysis of 64 Studies Involving 6000 Participants." *The British Psychological Society Research Digest*. December 7, 2018. https://digest.bps.org .uk/2018/12/07/meta-analysis-of-64-studies-involving-6000-participants-finds -that-self-explanation-is-a-powerful-learning-technique/ (accessed February 6, 2019).
34. Id.
35. Sieck, Winston. "Self-Explanation: A Good Reading Strategy for Bad Texts (& Good)." ThinkerAcademy.com (blog). January 3, 2019. https://thinkeracademy .com/self-explanation-reading-strategy/ (accessed February 6, 2019).
36. Kevin Arnovitz. "Pythons and PowerPonts: How the Sixers cracked the culture code." Apr 19, 2018. https://www.espn.com/nba/story/_/id/23216496/nba-how -philadelphia-76ers-formed-culture-built-win.
37. Id.
38. Dweck, Carol. *Mindset: The New Psychology of Success*, 16–17. New York City: Ballantine Books, 2006.
39. Id., at 25.

Chapter 2

1. Dorfman, Harvey. *The Mental ABCs of Pitching: A Handbook for Performance Enhancement*, at 91. Lanham, MD: The Rowman & Littlefield Publishing Group, Inc.
2. Clear, James. Interview with Ryan Hawk. *The Learning Leader Show*, "Episode 248: James Clear LIVE!—How Can We Live Better?" Podcast audio. March 11, 2018. https://learningleader.com/episode-248-james-clear-live-can-live-better/.
3. Goggins, David. Interview with Joe Rogan. *The Joe Rogan Experience*, "#1212— David Goggins." Podcast video, December 5, 2018. https://www.youtube.com /watch?v=BvWB7B8tXK8 (accessed December 19, 2018).
4. Lugavere, Max, and Paul Grewal. *Genius Foods: Become Smarter, Happier, and More Productive While Protecting Your Brain for Life*. New York City: HarperCollins Publishers, 2018.

5. Kurson, Robert. *Shadow Divers: The True Adventure of Two Americans Who Risked Everything to Solve One of the Lost Mysteries of World War II*, p. 35. New York City: Random House, 2005.

6. Savabe, Adam. Interview with Ryan Hawk. *The Learning Leader Show*, "Episode #311: Adam Savage: Life Lessons from a Master Maker." Podcast audio. May 18, 2019. http://bit.ly/savagehawk311.

7. O'Hagan, Sarah Robb. Interview with Ryan Hawk. *The Learning Leader Show*, "Episode 122: Sarah Robb O'Hagan—EXTREME YOU: Unlocking Your Potential." Podcast audio. May 8, 2016. https://learningleader.com/episode-122-sarah-robb-ohagan-extreme-you-unlocking-your-potential/.

8. Goodwin, Doris Kearns. *Leadership in Turbulent Times*. New York City: Simon & Schuster, 2018.

9. Id.

10. Parrish, Shane. "Decision Making: A Guide to Smarter Decisions and Reducing Errors." Farnam Street. n.d. https://fs.blog/smart-decisions/.

11. Drucker, Peter. *The Effective Executive: The Definitive Guide to Getting the Right Things Done*. New York City: HarperCollins Publishers, 1967.

12. Id.

13. Newport, Cal. *Deep Work: Rules for Focused Success in a Distracted World*. New York City: Grand Central Publishing, 2016.

14. McCullough, David. *The Wright Brothers*. Kindle version, p. 53. New York City: Simon & Schuster, 2016.

15. Ratey, John. *Spark: The Revolutionary New Science of Exercise and the Brain*. New York City: Little, Brown and Company, 2013.

16. "Study: Exercise Has Long-Lasting Effect on Depression." *Duke Today*. September 22, 2000. https://today.duke.edu/2000/09/exercise922.html (accessed December 4, 2018).

17. Roy, Brad. "Exercise and the Brain: More Reasons to Keep Moving." *American College of Sports Medicine's Health & Fitness Journal* 16, no. 5 (September/October, 2012). https://journals.lww.com/acsm-healthfitness/fulltext/2012/09000/Copy_and_Share__Exercise_and_the_Brain_More.3.aspx (accessed December 4, 2018).

18. Belsky, Scott. Personal Twitter feed. February 11, 2019. https://twitter.com/scottbelsky/status/1095051306589249536 (accessed February 16, 2019).

19. Peters, Tom. Personal Twitter feed. March 27, 2018. https://twitter.com/tom_peters/status/978670934159777792?lang=en (accessed March 18, 2019).

20. Useem. *The Leadership Moment*, 127 (Kindle ed.).

21. Luther, Claudia. "Coach John Wooden's Lesson on Shoes and Socks." UCLA Newsroom. June 4, 2010. http://newsroom.ucla.edu/stories/wooden-shoes-and-socks-84177 (accessed December 9, 2018).

22. Axelson, G. W. *Commy: The Life Story of Charles A. Comiskey*, at 316. Chicago: The Reilly & Lee Co., 2003.

Chapter 3

1. Coyle, Daniel. Interview with Ryan Hawk. *The Learning Leader Show*, "Episode 242: Daniel Coyle—The Secret of Highly Successful Groups (The Culture Code)." Podcast audio. January 28, 2018. http://learningleader.com/episode-242-daniel -coyle-secret-highly-successful-groups-culture-code/.
2. Geertz, Clifford. *The Interpretation of Cultures*. Basic Books, 2017.
3. Walsh, Bill, Steve Jamison, and Craig Walsh. *The Score Takes Care of Itself: My Philosophy of Leadership*, 25. New York: Portfolio, 2010.
4. Coyle, Daniel. *The Culture Code: The Secrets of Highly Successful Groups*. New York: Bantam Books, 2018.
5. D'Andrade, Roy. "The Cultural Part of Cognition." *Cognitive Science* 5, no. 3 (1981): 179–95. doi:10.1016/s0364-0213(81)80012-2.
6. Krasinski, John. Interview with Scott Feinberg. *Awards Chatter*, "John Krasinski ('A Quiet Place' & 'Jack Ryan'). Podcast audio. December 31, 2018. https://www .hollywoodreporter.com/race/awards-chatter-podcast-john-krasinski-a-quiet -place-1171612.
7. Ridge, Garry. Interview with Ryan Hawk. *The Learning Leader Show*, "Episode 125: Garry Ridge—How to Build a Tribal Culture (CEO WD-40)." Podcast audio. May 18, 2016. https://learningleader.com/episode-125-garry-ridge-how-to-build -a-tribal-culture-ceo-wd-40/.
8. Id.
9. Anderson, Chris. "TED's Secret to Great Public Speaking." March 2016. https:// www.ted.com/talks/chris_anderson_teds_secret_to_great_public_speaking /transcript?language=en (accessed March 23, 2019).
10. Id. (emphasis mine).
11. Economy, Peter. "Want Your Team's Respect and Loyalty? These 7 Habits Are Essential." *Inc.* https://www.inc.com/peter-economy/if-you-want-your-teams -respect-loyalty-these-7-habits-are-essential.html?cid=sf01001 (accessed November 26, 2018).
12. Pach, Chester J., Jr. "Dwight D. Eisenhower: Life Before the Presidency." UVA Miller Center. n.d. https://millercenter.org/president/eisenhower/life-before-the -presidency.
13. Id.
14. Myers, Joe. "Why Don't Employees Trust Their Bosses?" World Economic Forum. https://www.weforum.org/agenda/2016/04/why-dont-employees-trust-their -bosses/ (accessed July 26, 2018.)
15. Bingham, Sue. "If Employees Don't Trust You, It's Up to You to Fix It." *Harvard Business Review*. May 3, 2017. https://hbr.org/2017/01/if-employees-dont-trust -you-its-up-to-you-to-fix-it (accessed July 26, 2018).
16. Branson, Richard. Interview with Stephen Dubner. *Freakonomics*, "Extra: Richard Branson Full Interview (Ep. 321)." Podcast audio. February 25, 2018. http:// freakonomics.com/podcast/richard-branson/ (accessed July 26, 2018).

17. Id.
18. McChrystal, Stanley. "Listen, Learn . . . Then Lead." TED2011. March, 2011. https://www.ted.com/talks/stanley_mcchrystal/transcript#t-171738 (accessed March 24, 2019).
19. Id.
20. McChrystal, Stanley. Interview with Ryan Hawk. *The Learning Leader Show*, "Episode #303—General Stanley McChrystal—The New Definition of Leadership." Podcast audio. March 23, 2019. https://learningleader.com/mcchrystalhawk303/.
21. Jensen, Anabel. "Three Key Strategies from Stephen MR Covey: How to Lead with Trust & Optimize Wellbeing." Blog post. https://www.6seconds.org/2017/10/31/stephen-mr-covey-three-key-strategies/ (accessed March 24, 2019).
22. Id.
23. Id.
24. Cole, Kat. Interview with Ryan Hawk. *The Learning Leader Show*, "Episode 078: Kat Cole—From Hooters Waitress to President of Cinnabon." Podcast audio. December 7, 2015. https://learningleader.com/episode-078-kat-cole-from-hooters-waitress-to-president-of-cinnabon/.
25. Quinn, Brady. Interview with Ryan Hawk. *The Learning Leader Show*, "Episode 011: Brady Quinn—Why Certain People Are Great Leaders and Why Others Are Not." Podcast audio. May 24, 2016. http://learningleader.com/episode-011-brady-quinn-why-certain-people-are-great-leaders-and-why-others-are-not/.
26. Gallup, Inc. "How to Create a Culture of Psychological Safety." Gallup.com. December 7, 2017. https://news.gallup.com/opinion/gallup/223235/create-culture-psychological-safety.aspx (accessed July 26, 2018).
27. Duhigg, Charles. "What Google Learned from Its Quest to Build the Perfect Team." *New York Times*. February 25, 2016. https://www.nytimes.com/2016/02/28/magazine/what-google-learned-from-its-quest-to-build-the-perfect-team.html (accessed July 26, 2018).
28. Gallup, Inc. "How to Create a Culture of Psychological Safety." Gallup.com. December 7, 2017. https://news.gallup.com/opinion/gallup/223235/create-culture-psychological-safety.aspx (accessed July 26, 2018).
29. Seppälä and Cameron. "Proof That Positive Work Cultures Are More Productive."
30. Gallup, Inc. "How to Create a Culture of Psychological Safety." Gallup.com. December 07, 2017. https://news.gallup.com/opinion/gallup/223235/create-culture-psychological-safety.aspx (accessed July 26, 2018).
31. Marquet, David. Interview with Ryan Hawk. *The Learning Leader Show* "Episode #257: David Marquet—Intent Based Leadership (Turn The Ship Around!)." Podcast audio. May 13, 2018. http://learningleader.com/episode-257-david-marquet-intent-based-leadership-turn-ship-around/.
32. Seppälä and Cameron. "Proof That Positive Work Cultures Are More Productive."
33. Fussell, Chris. Interview with Ryan Hawk. *The Learning Leader Show*, "Episode 215: Chris Fussell—How to Build a Team of Teams (One Mission)." Podcast audio.

July 22, 2017. http://learningleader.com/episode-215-chris-fussell-build-team-teams-one-mission/.

34. Wojciechowski, Steve. Interview with Ryan Hawk. *The Learning Leader Show,* "Episode 226: Steve Wojciechowski—How to Win Every Day." Podcast audio. October 8, 2017. http://learningleader.com/episode-226-steve-wojciechowski-win-every-day/.

35. McChrystal, Stan. Interview with Ryan Hawk. *The Learning Leader Show,* "Episode #303: General Stanely McChrystal—The New Definition of Leadership.

36. Amabile, Teresa. Teresa Amabile's Progress Principle. http://www.progressprinciple.com/ (accessed July 30, 2018).

37. Cloud, Henry. Interview with Ryan Hawk. *The Learning Leader Show,* "Episode 229: Henry Cloud—'Be So Good They Can't Ignore You.'" Podcast audio. October 29, 2017. http://learningleader.com/episode-229-henry-cloud-good-cant-ignore/.

38. Greene, Robert. Interview with Ryan Hawk. *The Learning Leader Show,* "Episode 220: Robert Greene—The Laws of Power & Mastery." Podcast audio. August 26, 2017. https://learningleader.com/episode-220-robert-greene-laws-power-mastery/.

39. Wiseman, Liz. Interview with Ryan Hawk. *The Learning Leader Show,* "Episode 160: Liz Wiseman—Why Lack of Experience Is Your Advantage." Podcast audio. September 20, 2016. http://learningleader.com/episode-160-liz-wiseman/.

Chapter 4

1. Collins, Jim. Interview with Ryan Hawk. *The Learning Leader Show,* "Episode 216: Jim Collins—How to Go from Good to Great." Podcast audio. July 30, 2017. https://learningleader.com/episode-216-jim-collins-go-good-great/.

2. Useem, Michael. *The Leadership Moment. Nine Stories of Triumph and Disaster and Their Lesson for Us All,* at 88 (Kindle ed.). New York City: Crown Business, 1999.

3. Id.

4. Eisner, Michael, and Aaron Cohen. *Working Together: Why Great Partnerships Succeed,* at 49 (Kindle ed.). New York City: HarperBusiness, 2012.

5. McChrystal, Stanley. Interview with Ryan Hawk. *The Learning Leader Show,* "Episode #303: General Stanley McChrystal—The New Definition of Leadership." March 23, 2019. https://learningleader.com/mcchrystalhawk303/.

6. Watkins, Michael. Interview with Ryan Hawk. *The Learning Leader Show,* "Episode 180: Michael Watkins—The First 90 Days: How to Ensure Success in Your New Role." Podcast audio. December 12, 2016. https://learningleader.com/episode-180-michael-watkins-first-90-days-ensure-success-new-role/.

7. "Lessons from Keith Rabois Essay 2: How to Interview an Executive." April 12, 2019. www.delian.io/lessons-2.

8. Bryant, Kobe. Personal twitter feed. December 12, 2014. https://twitter.com/kobebryant/status/543472541285629952?lang=en (acccessed March 29, 2019).

9. Clifton, Jim, and Jim Harter. *It's the Manager*. Gallup Press, 2019. Also discussed in Clifton, Jim. Interview with Ryan Hawk. *The Learning Leader Show*, "Episode #319: Jim Clifton—How to Become a World-Class Manager (CEO of Gallup)." Podcast audio. July 9, 2019. https://learningleader.com/cliftonhawk319/.

10. Gordon, Jon. Interview with Ryan Hawk. *The Learning Leader Show*, "Episode 072: Jon Gordon—Optimistic People Win More | The Energy Bus." Podcast audio. November 16, 2015. https://learningleader.com/episode-072-jon-gordon -optimistic-people-win-more-the-energy-bus/.

11. Sinek, Simon. Interview with Ryan Hawk. *The Learning Leader Show*, "Episode 107: Simon Sinek—Leadership: It Starts with Why." Podcast audio. March 16, 2016. https://learningleader.com/episode-107-simon-sinek-leadership-it-starts -with-why/.

12. Kerr, James. Interview with Ryan Hawk. *The Learning Leader Show*, "Episode #301: James Kerr—How to Create an Ethos of Excellence (Legacy)." Podcast audio. March 10, 2019. https://learningleader.com/kerrhawk301/.

13. Wilner, Barry. "All 12 Playoff Coaches Are Tied to Bill Walsh or Parcells." *Star-Tribune*. January 5, 2019. http://www.startribune.com/all-12-playoff-coaches-are -tied-to-bill-walsh-or-parcells/503940492/ (accessed March 23, 2019).

Chapter 5

1. "USA Cycling Hires New Balance Boss Rob DeMartini as CEO." ESPN.com. January 7, 2019. http://www.espn.com/olympics/cycling/story/_/id/25706319/usa-cycling-hires-new-balance-boss-rob-demartini-ceo (accessed February 16, 2019).

2. DeMartini, Rob. Interview with Ryan Hawk. *The Learning Leader Show*, "Episode 042: Rob DeMartini—CEO of New Balance: The Leader Behind Their Explosive Growth." Podcast audio. August 2, 2015. https://learningleader.com/episode-042 -rob-demartini-ceo-of-new-balance-the-leader-behind-their-explosive-growth/.

3. Brown, Brené. "The Power of Vulnerability." TEDxHouston. 2010. https://www .ted.com/talks/brene_brown_on_vulnerability?language=en.

4. Rutledge, Pamela. "The Psychological Power of Storytelling." *Psychology Today* (blog). January 16, 2011. https://www.psychologytoday.com/us/blog/positively -media/201101/the-psychological-power-storytelling (accessed February 17, 2019).

5. Gionek, Katie L., and Paul E. King. "Listening to Narratives: An Experimental Examination of Storytelling in the Classroom." Taylor & Francis Online. January 8, 2014. https://www.tandfonline.com/doi/abs/10.1080/10904018.2014.861302 ?journalCode=hijl20 (accessed July 27, 2018).

6. Snow, Shane. *SmartCuts: How Hackers, Innovators, and Icons Accelerate Success*, p. 6 (Kindle edition). New York: HarperCollins Publishers Inc., 2014.

7. Id., p. 13.

8. http://www.billhicks.com/quotes.html.

9. Weinberger, Matt. "Elon Musk Reportedly Tells Tesla Employees That They Should Just Leave Meetings or Hang up the Phone If It's Not Productive." *Business*

Insider. April 17, 2018. https://www.businessinsider.com/elon-musk-productivity
-tip-leave-meetings-if-theyre-not-productive-2018-4 (accessed July 26, 2018).

10. Trask, Amy. Interview with Ryan Hawk. *The Learning Leader Show*, Episode 163:
Amy Trask—Former NFL CEO: "You Negotiate Like a Girl." Podcast audio. September 28, 2016. https://learningleader.com/?s=amy+trask.

11. Yeh, Raymond T., and Stephanie H. Yeh. *The Art of Business: In the Footsteps of
Giants*, p. 143. Olathe, CO: Zero Time Publishing, 2004.

12. Zenger, Jack, and Joseph Folkman. "What Great Listeners Actually Do." *Harvard Business Review.* July 14, 2016. https://hbr.org/2016/07/what-great-listeners
-actually-do (accessed July 26, 2018).

13. Cialdini, Robert. Interview with Ryan Hawk. *The Learning Leader Show*, "Episode
167: Robert Cialdini—The Godfather of Influence." Podcast audio. October 12,
2016. https://learningleader.com/episode-167-robert-cialdini-godfather-influence/.

14. Peters, Tom, and Robert H. Waterman. *In Search of Excellence: Lessons from
America's Best-Run Companies.* Sydney NSW: Harper & Row Publishers, 1984.

15. "The Daily Show's Writers' Room Exemplifies 'Burstiness.'" Cheddar. June 6,
2018. https://cheddar.com/videos/the-daily-shows-writers-room-exemplifies
-burstiness (accessed July 26, 2018).

16. McMahan, Charlie. Interview with Ryan Hawk. *The Learning Leader Show*, "Episode #263: Charlie McMahan—How to Build a Tribe from 50 to 5,000." Podcast
audio. June 24, 2018. https://learningleader.com/charliemcmahansouthbrook/.

17. Scott, Kim Malone. Interview with Ryan Hawk. *The Learning Leader Show*, "Episode 223: Kim Malone Scott—Using Radical Candor to Be a Great Boss." Podcast
audio. September 17, 2017. http://learningleader.com/episode-223-kim-malone
-scott-using-radical-candor-great-boss/.

18. Brian Koppelman. Twitter feed. June 4, 2018. https://twitter.com/briankoppelman
/status/1003435779811618816 (accessed July 26, 2018).

19. Graham, Paul. "Maker's Schedule, Manager's Schedule." (blog). July 2009. http://
www.paulgraham.com/makersschedule.html (accessed February 20, 2019).

20. Mueller, Pam A., and Daniel M. Oppenheimer. "The Pen Is Mightier Than the
Keyboard: Advantages of Longhand Over Laptop Note Taking." Psychological Science OnlineFirst, published on May 22, 2014, as doi:10.1177/0956797614524581.

Chapter 6

1. Kerr, James. Interview with Ryan Hawk. *The Learning Leader Show*, "Episode
#301: James Kerr—How to Create an Ethos of Excellence (Legacy)." Podcast audio.
March 10, 2019. https://learningleader.com/kerrhawk301/.

2. Peters, Tom. Personal twitter feed. February 6, 2018. https://twitter.com/tom
_peters/status/960984439470702597 (accessed April 3, 2019).

3. Michael Useem. Interview with Ryan Hawk. *The Learning Leader Show*, "Episode
#298: Michael Useem—How To Become A Learning Machine." Podcast audio.
February 17, 2019. https://learningleader.com/useemhawk298/.

4. Peters, Tom. "More Management Misconceptions." Personal blog post. Date unknown. https://tompeters.com/columns/more-management-misconceptions/ (accessed April 4, 2019).

5. Greene, Robert. *The 33 Strategies of War*. London: Profile Books LTD.

6. Id.

7. Id.

8. Buckingham, Marcus. Interview with Ryan Hawk. *The Learning Leader Show*, "Episode #305: Marcus Buckingham & Ashley Goodall—A Leader's Guide to the Real World (Break All the Rules)." Podcast audio. April 5, 2019. https://learningleader.com/buckinghamhawk305/.

9. Venus, Merlijn, Daan Stam, and Daan van Knippenberg. "Research: To Get People to Embrace Change, Emphasize What Will Stay the Same." *Harvard Business Review*. August 15, 2018. https://hbr.org/2018/08/research-to-get-people -to-embrace-change-emphasize-what-will-stay-the-same (accessed March 19, 2019).

10. Useem, Michael. *The Leadership Moment*.

11. Sivers, Derek. Personal blog post. January 28, 2019. https://sivers.org/dj (accessed February 17, 2019).

12. Guidara, Will. Interview with Brian Koppelman. *The Moment with Brian Koppelman*. "Will Guidara 2/12/19." Podcast audio. February 12, 2019. https://www .stitcher.com/podcast/the-moment-with-brian-koppelman/e/58729476 (accessed February 17, 2019).

13. Jones, Phil. Interview with Ryan Hawk. *The Learning Leader Show*, "Episode #221: Phil Jones—What to Say to Influence and Impact Others (Magic Words)." Podcast audio. September 3, 2017. https://learningleader.com/episode-221-phil-jones-say -influence-impact-others-magic-words/.

14. Walsh, Bill. *The Score Takes Care of Itself*, at 30.

15. Kerr, James. Interview with Ryan Hawk. *The Learning Leader Show*, "Episode #301: James Kerr—How to Create an Ethos of Excellence (Legacy). Podcast audio. March 10, 2019. https://learningleader.com/kerrhawk301/.

16. Gregorek, Jerzy. Interview with Tim Ferriss. *The Tim Ferriss Show*. "The Lion of Olympic Weightlifting, 62-Year-Old Jerzy Gregorek (Also Featuring: Naval Ravikant) (#228)." Podcast audio. March 16, 2017. https://tim.blog/2017/03/16 /jerzy-gregorek/ (accessed November 28, 2018).

17. Marcinko, Richard. "Quotable Quote." Goodreads.com. https://www.goodreads .com/quotes/121087-the-more-you-sweat-in-training-the-less-you-bleed (accessed March 25, 2019).

18. Becker, Joshua. "The Hidden Power of Humility." Personal blog post. Date unknown. https://www.becomingminimalist.com/the-hidden-power-of -humility/ (accessed March 23, 2019).

19. Koppelman, Brian. Interview with Ryan Hawk. *The Learning Leader Show*, "Episode #306: Brian Koppelman—Follow Your Curiosity and Obsessions with Rigor." Podcast audio. April 14, 2019. https://learningleader.com/koppelmanhawk/.

20. Beshore, Brent. Interview with Ryan Hawk. *The Learning Leader Show*, "Episode #293: Brent Beshore—How to Get Rich Slow & Live an Optimal Life." Podcast audio. January 12, 2019. https://learningleader.com/beshorehawk/.

Conclusion

1. Liddell, H. G., and R. Scott. *A Greek–English Lexicon*, 9th ed. Oxford, 1940. s.v. ἀρετή. Cited in Wikipedia, *"Arete."*

2. Fiorina, Carly. Interview with Ryan Hawk. *The Learning Leader Show*, "Episode #307: Carly Fiorina—Why You Should Run Towards the Fire." Podcast audio, April 21, 2019. https://learningleader.com/fiorinahawk307/.

3. Band, Zvi. Interview with Ryan Hawk. *The Learning Leader Show*, "Episode #312: Zvi Band—How to Leverage the Power of Your Relationships. Podcast audio. May 25, 2019. https://learningleader.com/bandhawk312/.

4. Redick, J. J. Interview with Ryan Hawk. *The Learning Leader Show*, "Episode #217: J. J. Redick—'You've Never Arrived. You're Always Becoming.'" Podcast audio. August 6, 2017. https://learningleader.com/episode-217-jj-redick-youve-never-arrived-youre-always-becoming/

INDEX

ABOUT THE AUTHOR

Ryan Hawk is a keynote speaker, author, advisor, and the host of *The Learning Leader Show*, which *Forbes* called "the most dynamic leadership podcast out there" and *Inc.* magazine recognized on its list of "5 Podcasts to Make You a Smarter Leader." Featuring interviews with hundreds of bestselling authors and world-renowned corporate, athletic, and military leaders, the show has millions of listeners in more than 150 countries.

As head of Brixey & Meyer's leadership advisory practice, Ryan speaks regularly at Fortune 500 companies, works with teams and players in the NFL, NBA, and NCAA, and facilitates Leadership Circles that offer structured guidance and collaborative feedback to new and experienced leaders.

Ryan was a high school, college, and professional quarterback and captain. When he transitioned to the corporate world, he advanced professionally from award-winning individual contributor to vice president of sales for a multibillion-dollar company.

A lifelong student of leadership, Ryan draws upon his experiences, empirical evidence, and expert insights to strive for continuous improvement in his own life and to inspire other leaders to achieve and sustain excellence. He is passionate about helping others to become humble servant leaders who build committed organizations, as intentionally and painlessly as possible.

For more information about Ryan Hawk, visit LearningLeader.com.